THE VOICE-ACTIVATED CLASSROOM

Recode Your Classroom's DNA With the Power of Words

Dr. LaKesa Bradford – Mitchell

KINGDOM STYLE LIVING, LLC

I0540287

Copyright © 2025 by LaKesa Bradford Mitchell

All rights reserved.

No part of this book may be reproduced, stored in a retrieval system, or transmitted in any form or by any means—electronic, mechanical, photocopying, recording, or otherwise—without the prior written permission of the publisher, except for brief quotations used in reviews or scholarly works.

This book is a work of non-fiction. Unless otherwise noted, the author and the publisher make no explicit guarantees as to the accuracy of the information contained in this book and in some cases, names of people and places have been altered to protect their privacy.

The Voice-Activated Classroom: Recode Your Classroom's DNA with the Power of Words

ISBN: 9798218653019 (sc)
ISBN: 9798218482572 (hc)
ISBN: 9798218482589 (e)

Published by Kingdom Style Living, LLC.
Baton Rouge, LA.

Cover design and interior layout by Katarina
Printed in the United States of America

For more information, visit: www.lakesabradfordmitchell.com

This book is a work of nonfiction. Names, situations, and events referenced are either based on the author's experiences or used with permission. Any resemblance to actual persons or events is purely coincidental unless otherwise stated.

First Edition: 2025

"Children are a blessing and a gift from the Lord"

PSALM 127:3 CEV

CONTENTS

APPENDIX 141

The Day Words Changed My Life

-⁓ⱮⱮⱮⱮ⁓

M y journey toward understanding the immense power of words in rewiring the brain started with a pivotal experience of my own. Here was a moment in my life when a teacher's words left an indelible mark, changing how I saw myself and what I believed I could achieve. It was a moment that would set me on the path to becoming an educator and eventually writing this book. Allow me to share this story with you, as it shows how a single phrase can echo across a lifetime and lead to a passion for helping others harness the transformative power of their words.

It was early in the 1980s. The River Parish School System was nearing the end of its first year of launch of the brand-new magnet program at McCallister Middle Magnet School. This day, however, was a bit different than any other in my fifth-grade classroom. It was the day that my teacher, Mrs. X, was going to announce which students had been selected to attend the new magnet school the next year. Mrs. X built eagerness by telling the class about all the new and interesting courses and electives that would be afforded to us if we were chosen. I was excited when Mrs. X mentioned that there would be dance and typing classes. I liked to dance, and I'd always wanted to learn how to type.

Later in her speech, Mrs. X told the class that we would each receive a letter to take home to our parents that would explain why a student was or was not chosen for the magnet school program. Reasons such as a student's grades and score on the CAT (California Achievement Test) weighed in on the selection criteria. Students were also chosen through teacher recommendation.

I stared at the envelope addressed to "The Parents of LaKesa Bradford." I waited until the school bell rang before I tore it open and read the letter. "Not Accepted" were the words that stood out to me the most. I was disappointed to learn that I wasn't selected to attend the prestigious middle magnet school, but the crushing moment hadn't occurred yet. The crushing moment came when I asked Mrs. X to tell me why I wasn't chosen to attend the magnet school.

"Mrs. X," I said, "Why didn't I get picked to go?"

"LaKesa, you didn't get chosen because you ain't magnet material, my dear," she replied.

I didn't even know what that meant, but the way my teacher said it assured me that it was synonymous with not being good enough. She said it so matter-of-factly, as if she was sure that I would never be good enough, not then, nor ever. It was the first time in my ten-year-old life that I had been made to feel flawed and mediocre by an adult. No adult had ever told me that I wasn't good enough. Kids said mean things on the playground, but this was different because it came from an adult.

My body posture and teary eyes told all my friends that I didn't get chosen. Everyone now knew that instead of going to what we had named "the smart school" next school year, I would be going to the school where, in my eyes, "regular" kids went, and I didn't want to be regular.

When my mom found out that Mrs. X told me that I wasn't "magnet material," she was livid, to say the least. I was a B–C student, but that didn't give her the right to tell me what I wasn't, nor the right to define what material I was made from. My mom took my teacher's statement personally.

I grew up in a household where my mom and dad believed in speaking life into me and my sisters. We were constantly told that we were beautiful, smart, and that we could become anything we wanted in life. On a regular basis, my parents taught my sisters and I to recite scriptures that reminded us of who we were, scriptures such as "I have the mind of Christ" (1 Corinthians 2:16, KJV) and "I am the head and not the tail" (Deuteronomy 28:13, KJV). I grew up in a household where I wasn't told what I wasn't; I was told what I was. So perhaps you can see why my teacher's statement was unusual to my tender ears.

I later realized that not all kids are afforded the same opportunity to grow up in a household where parents speak life into them. Some kids grow up in households where parents talk down to them, say belittling words, or compare them to unsuccessful members of their family and predict their future to be the same. My heart goes out to the children who don't have anyone at home or a teacher at school who believes in them.

My mom told me to begin saying, "I am magnet material." I was now on a quest to align my actions with my words. I created a list of life-producing phrases that I would speak into the atmosphere each day. Phrases such as "I can comprehend, retain, and apply the concepts that I am being taught." In that pivotal moment, the words I spoke to myself began to reshape my identity and purpose as a student. What had once been self-doubt and hesitation transformed into motivation and focus. With every life-producing phrase, I was rewriting my narrative and shifting from limitations to possibilities. Those words of belief and determination started a domino effect, improving my academic behavior and inspiring me to push through challenges. This was how I began to recode my own DNA—not in a biological sense, but in the essence of who I was becoming. That shift became the foundation for a lifelong journey, proving that the power of words could not only change my behavior but also ignite my potential.

My fifth-grade school year ended, and summer was in full swing. I was officially a sixth-grade student. By that time, my mom had done a bit of calling around, research, and praying. She found out that at the end of my first semester in sixth grade, if I earned a 4.0, I would be admitted to the new magnet school. A 4.0 GPA? Straight A's? Not one B or C? I had never earned straight A's before, but I was determined to do it. I accepted this challenge for one reason: to prove to myself that I was indeed "magnet material."

In August, I began middle school with a mission. My mission was to simply become what I was told I wasn't: "magnet material." I don't remember much about the semester, but I do remember receiving a note from the cutest guy in sixth grade. The note read, "Do you like me? Check the box (yes or no)." I politely wrote a note in reply, "Dear Taurus, I really like you, but I cannot have a boyfriend right now because I am focusing on my grades." I was so determined to become magnet material that I wouldn't even entertain the cutest boy in the whole sixth grade.

By the time mid-December rolled around, I was at the end of the first semester of sixth grade. I'd endured many long and late nights studying for tests and writing essays, and I spent many nights crying. Not because I couldn't do the work or because it was too hard; I cried because, like any athlete in training, I had to endure the uncomfortable process of getting to the stage of performance needed to be successful in the new season. The more the athlete works out his body, the easier the process will become, until the bar is set higher. I likened myself to an athlete, except I was training my mind. I was in an unfamiliar place, a place where average was no longer acceptable for me. My mom can attest that any time I scored less than an A on an assignment, I would cry. I would redo assignments if they weren't completed to an A standard. I put a lot of pressure on myself and missed a lot of neighborhood playtime with my friends, but I was also determined to become magnet material.

All my teachers and friends knew that I was working hard to earn straight A's, and everyone was cheering for me. On the last day of final exams, I brought a grade form to each of my teachers so that they could write in my final grade for the semester. This was the form that I would need to take to the middle magnet school to be granted admission into its program.

As I made my way to my first teacher's class, I held my breath as she wrote down my grade of an A and signed her name next to it. I slowly exhaled and smiled as I read the added comment, "Great job, LaKesa!"

My second, third, and fourth-hour teachers each wrote the letter grade that I'd earned in their class: A. By the time I'd made it to my sixth-hour class, I'd picked up a crowd of students who followed me to the teacher's desk as he wrote in my letter grade: A.

The crowd became as engulfed in this process as I was. When I held my breath, they held their breath. When I smiled, they smiled and cheered me on. I was especially empowered to read other teacher comments such as "hard worker," "did excellent work," and my favorite: "so proud of you."

Seventh hour, the last class of the day, was the grade that would be the determining factor in my acceptance into the magnet school program. I must say, I was nervous about this grade because math was not my strongest subject. My heart was beating fast, and I wasn't sure if I wanted the crowd to gather around me for this one. Nevertheless, I handed the teacher my grade form, and to my surprise, I'd earned an A.

I screamed, the crowd screamed, and someone even picked me up and spun me around. I did it! For the first time ever, I'd earned straight A's. It was my greatest victory yet. I realized it wasn't that I hadn't been smart enough to earn straight A's before; it was that I had never been pushed to do it. I could not hold back the tears of joy; this accomplishment meant that I would finally be granted admission into the very school that my teacher said I wasn't good enough to attend.

My mom was waiting for me in the school office to check me out and take me to my new school to register. She was thrilled to see my report card and echoed words of praise, but I could tell by the look on her face that something else was on her mind. We climbed into the car and drove to the destination that my mom had in mind: Westchester Elementary School, which was my former elementary school. I had no idea why we were there, but I would soon find out.

"Mom, why did we come back here?" I asked.

"'Cause, before we turn this report card in to the new magnet school, you gon' sho' Mrs. X this report card and tell her butt that you are magnet material!"

I did exactly what my momma told me to do that day. In fact, for several more report cards that I received at the magnet school, my momma would drive me back to Westchester Elementary School to show my fifth-grade teacher my honor roll grades.

I remained an honor roll student throughout high school, and I was even inducted into the National Beta Club. These accomplishments were not easy by any means! I continued to stay up late to study, and I cried when things were difficult. Through all of this, I learned perseverance and fortitude. If it wasn't for that life-defining moment in my fifth-grade class, I am not sure if I would have pushed myself to stimulate the unused potential inside of me. Sure, my parents encouraged me and spoke life into me, but my fifth-grade teacher, indirectly, by telling me that I wasn't good enough, made me realize that there were dormant and undeveloped capabilities inside of me. I realized that every person is born with greatness inside of them because we all have the same creator, but I also realized that there is greatness buried in millions of graves across this world.

I became an educator because I was on a mission to positively influence the lives of as many students as I was graced to teach, lead, and inspire. I vowed never to tell a child what they were not capable of achieving but to use my words to uplift, inspire, and activate the dormant possibilities in children. I named my class "Bradford's Believers." Every morning, my students and I started each day with positive, life-producing phrases. The transformation in their confidence and academic performance was remarkable. Seeing the results of the Voice-Activated approach, I reinforced my commitment to the framework. As a teacher, my classrooms became Voice-Activated Classrooms. As an elementary, middle, and high school principal, my campuses became Voice-Activated campuses.

LaKesa Bradford / 5th gd.

INTRODUCTION

Words build worlds and voices cast vision. This is why, as educators, we hold the sacred honor of igniting destinies, serving as catalysts for vision, and activating untapped potential – through the words spoken by the individuals in the classroom. In every classroom, words are world-builders, vision-shapers, and destiny-igniters.

This book isn't just about how you speak to your students. It's about how your students speak to themselves, to each other, and into the atmosphere around them.

This is not just another book about classroom management. This is a book about recoding. A blueprint. A reawakening of the most underestimated superpower in education: **your voice**.

You picked up this book because, deep down, you know there's more to teaching than test prep and discipline referrals. You know that your students are more than their behavior charts, and you are more than a manager of chaos. You are a *culture creator,* a *mindset shifter,* and a *dream defender.* You're on the front lines—fighting to keep your students engaged, motivated, and emotionally safe while also meeting state standards, calming parents, and staying sane.

So why does it feel like you're losing ground?

We don't just need better systems. We need better sound.

Because for too long, we've underestimated the true power of language in the classroom. And that ends now.

From the very beginning, it was not movement that created matter—it was voice. A sound cut through silence: "Let there be..." and the universe obeyed. Light emerged. Life began. Purpose took shape. All because something was spoken.

And the same divine law still governs our world today—especially in our classrooms.

Every classroom is a living environment: voice-activated, sound-responsive, and atmosphere-sensitive. It is not shaped by curriculum alone, or test scores, or even the decor on the walls. It is shaped by the collective words spoken inside it, by every voice that enters through its doors.

Yes, the teacher's words matter. They lead. They model. They plant seeds of belief or doubt. But so do the students' words—spoken to themselves, to each other, and back to the world. Together, their voices create the climate. Together, they build or break the culture.

This is the unspoken truth of education: the classroom becomes what is said within it. When a teacher speaks life, a student stands taller. When a peer speaks kindness, a wall begins to fall. When a student speaks confidence over their own ability, a new neural path is paved.

But when sarcasm becomes the norm...

When shame is spoken casually...

When students learn to silence themselves before they've even begun—

The atmosphere dims.

The classroom shrinks.

And learning suffocates.

This is not just about positive reinforcement. This is about brain development. Identity formation. Mental health. Legacy. Rekindling deferred dreams. Because the words we speak don't just

echo in the moment—they echo in memory. In mindset. In the mirror of how students see themselves.

Beneath the surface of every classroom is something deeper—something unseen but always present. Like the invisible code embedded in every living organism, there is a code within the culture of every classroom. It's what I call Classroom DNA. This DNA is not made up of cells, but of sound. Not nucleotides, but names, narratives, and norms. It is built strand by strand through the language patterns we model, the belief systems we vocalize, and the expectations we repeat. It is formed through tone, through timing, through repetition, and through relationship.

Classroom DNA

DNA is the blueprint that shapes every human body; in the same way, every classroom has its own blueprint too. No two bodies are identical, and neither are any two classrooms. Just as the human body's double helix DNA model *(Figure 1)* serves as the blueprint for life, encoding genetic instructions that determine growth, development, and function, the Voice-Activated Classroom's double helix model *(Figure 2)* serves as the foundational structure for shaping a thriving learning environment.

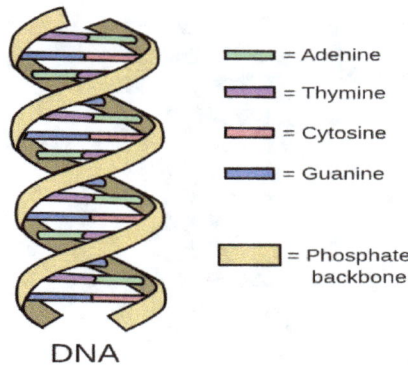

Figure 1: Human Body DNA Model

Each strand of DNA contains sequences of bases that, when activated, influence biological traits, and likewise, strands of Voice-Activated Classroom DNA are made up of interconnected bases, each representing an individual voice within the classroom and its paired role in speaking life-producing words. When spoken into the atmosphere, these words shape student mindsets, engagement, and academic performance. This model suggests that just as DNA expression can be influenced by environmental factors—a concept explored in epigenetics—classroom culture can be transformed when teachers and students intentionally use forward-thinking, igniting, and expectation-driven language that activates students' potential. By rewiring the "genetic code" of the classroom through intentional speech, educators can fundamentally shift students' neural pathways, cognitive habits, and self-belief, effectively recoding the DNA of their learning experience.

VOICE - ACTIVATED CLASSROOM FRAMEWORK

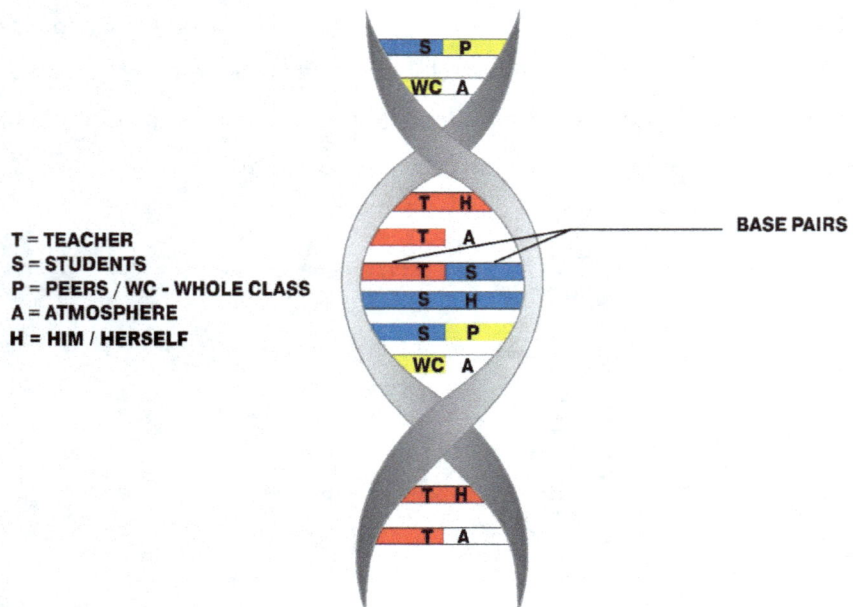

T = TEACHER
S = STUDENTS
P = PEERS / WC - WHOLE CLASS
A = ATMOSPHERE
H = HIM / HERSELF

Figure 2: Voice-Activated Classroom Model

The double helix structure of the Voice-Activated Classroom consists of two interwoven strands: the Teacher's Voice and the Student's Voice. These strands are inseparably linked, continuously influencing and reinforcing one another. The Teacher's Voice strand represents the intentional words and belief-infused statements that educators speak into the classroom atmosphere. These words serve as catalysts, activating confidence, engagement, and intellectual curiosity in students. The Student's Voice strand represents how students internalize, adopt, and eventually verbalize the language modeled by their teacher, transforming their self-perception and peer interactions. These two strands twist and reinforce each other through daily life-producing phrases, structured classroom dialogue, and consistent verbal reinforcement of growth-oriented beliefs. Just as DNA replication ensures continuity and adaptation in living organisms, the Voice-Activated Classroom's language patterns replicate and evolve within students, equipping them with a self-sustaining framework of positive self-talk and academic resilience that extends beyond the classroom walls.

What Are Voice-Activated Classrooms?

Voice-Activated Classrooms are classrooms ignited by powerful, life-producing words and unlimited beliefs. More specifically, Voice-Activated Classrooms are:

> *Classrooms led by teachers who believe in the power of their words and the ability to use those words to unlock the enormous potential inside of each student. In a Voice-Activated Classroom, individuals within the classroom all use their voices for purpose.*

In a Voice-Activated Classroom, intentional, verbal, declarative phrases are announced into the atmosphere through six (6) different conduits.

The conduits make up the six strands of the Voice-Activated Classroom's DNA:

"A" Strand		"B" Strand	
	Teacher		Him/Herself
	Teacher		Atmosphere
	Teacher		Student(s)
	Student(s)		Him/Herself
	Student(s)		Peers
	Whole Class		Atmosphere

Figure 3: Voice-Activated Classroom Chart

The Voice-Activated Classroom is based on connections within the environment. When the bases of the "A" Strand are intentionally paired with the bases of the "B" Strand, a powerful chain reaction is set in motion, activating a learning environment rooted in purpose, connection, and life-giving words.

▶ Connection 1: Teacher examines / recodes internal dialogue.
▶ Connection 2: Teacher examines / recodes the atmosphere of the classroom.
▶ Connection 3: Teacher examines / recodes their words to the students.
▶ Connection 4: Students examine / recode their internal dialogue.
▶ Connection 5: Students examine / recode their words to their peers.
▶ Connection 6: The Whole Class examines / recodes the atmosphere of the classroom.

Each of these six (6) Base Pair Connections will be unpacked in the chapters that follow, offering practical guidance and real classroom examples to help you activate and apply them with intention and confidence.

Other definitions:

▶ **Voice-Activated School Campus:** A campus where over half of the classrooms are ignited by powerful words and unlimited beliefs.

▶ **Voice-Activated School District:** A school district where over half of the school campuses in the district are ignited by powerful words and unlimited beliefs.

Why This Book Matters Now

Here's the truth: students are drowning in negative input. From social media, music, trauma, unstable home environments, and even the hallways of their school, they are fed a steady diet of words that tell them they're not enough. And when they don't hear a better voice, they begin to believe the worst ones. There is an urgency for every district, campus, and classroom leader to increase the feeling of community, inclusivity, and empowerment now.

That's why this book doesn't just focus on what *the adults* say. It equips adults to teach students how to speak—*to themselves, to each other, and into their own futures.* When students learn to use life-producing words, they stop tearing each other down and start building one another up. They stop quitting on themselves and start activating the mindset required to grow.

What would happen if every student in your classroom felt like they truly belonged, were fully welcomed, trusted the people around them, and were encouraged to rise to every challenge—every single day?

That's the kind of environment The Voice-Activated Classroom helps you create—because when students feel safe, seen, and supported, learning isn't just possible... it's optimized.

Why I'm the One to Write This

Because I've lived every angle of it.

I'm a former school principal and classroom teacher, with over 30 years of experience in urban, under-resourced, high-demand schools. I've worked with students written off by others, and I've witnessed the transformation that happens when teachers shift their language and students find their own voice.

More personally, I *was* that student. In fifth grade, I was told I wasn't smart enough to belong in a school for high-achievers. One sentence rewired my confidence. But years later, recoding words restored it. That experience shaped everything I've done as an educator—and it's the fire behind every page you're about to read.

This book is built on evidence and experience. On neuroscience and pedagogy. On heart and results. And on the unshakable belief that every teacher and student carries the power to speak life—and change lives.

Let's Address the Elephant in the Room

You might be thinking:

▶ "These kids don't respond unless you come at them a certain way."

▶ "I don't have time for fluff—I've got standards to teach."

▶ "It's too late to fix this group. They don't even talk respectfully to *each other*."

But let me challenge you: What if the way forward isn't through more control... but through more connection?

What if what's missing isn't toughness, but *training in how to talk differently?*

This isn't about softening expectations. This is about *strengthening connection*. And this framework works—even with the students you've already labeled "unreachable." When teachers speak life, students begin to mirror it. When students speak life to themselves and their peers, the culture shifts from the inside out.

What You'll Find in This Book

This book is loaded with:

▶ **Practical steps** and immediately actionable strategies aligned to national teacher observation rubrics. Easy to implement without needing to overhaul your curriculum or add another task to your plate.

▶ **Real-world success stories** from classrooms just like yours, where the power of intentional speech turned everything around.

▶ **Original prayers** and declarations written specifically for educators—for those days when you need divine strength, clarity, patience, or all three at once.

▶ **A framework** that is research-backed, SEL-aligned, and proven in some of the toughest educational spaces.

You'll be empowered to:

▶ Awaken the unmotivated student.

▶ Create the ultimate "bully-free", culturally safe environment.

▶ Empower students to dream again.

▶ Use language to activate social-emotional growth.

▶ Teach your students to speak life—to themselves and to each other.

Let me be clear: this is not a book you just *read*.

This is a book that *changes*.

A book that *activates.*

A book that *includes everyone.*

Because when your voice changes, your classroom begins to heal.
When their voice is activated, the atmosphere becomes electric.
And when everyone is speaking life, learning becomes unstoppable.

Let's activate it. Together.

Part I

THE
STRUCTURE

"Just like DNA carries instructions for life, the language we use in the classroom writes the blueprint for how students see themselves and what they believe they are capable of."

-Dr. LaKesa (TEDxJesterCirED, 2025)

THE 1ST BASE PAIR

Teacher : Him/Herself

VOICE - ACTIVATED CLASSROOM FRAMEWORK

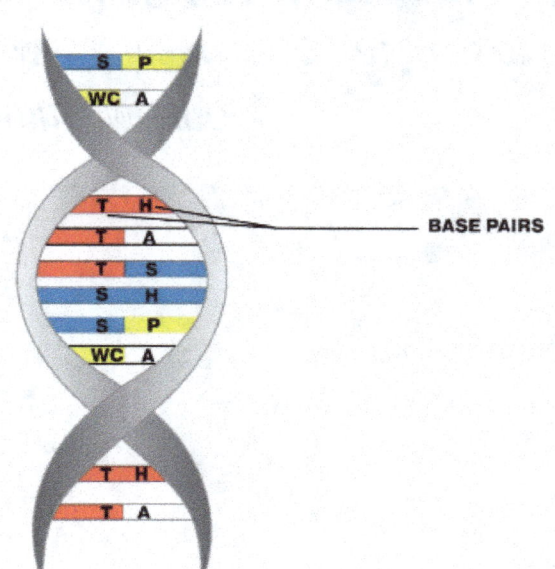

T = TEACHER
S = STUDENTS
P = PEERS / WC - WHOLE CLASS
A = ATMOSPHERE
H = HIM / HERSELF

BASE PAIRS

Your life--and your classroom--will always follow the direction of your most dominant thoughts and your most repeated words...So, if you want to change the narrative of your classroom, you must first rewrite the narrative in your own mind.

CHAPTER 1

TEACHER REWIRED

Teacher: Him/Herself

S tart with you.

If the teacher's inner language is broken, the classroom will be too.

Mrs. Anderson

The room was alive with the chatter of students, a symphony of youthful energy that could either inspire or overwhelm. Mrs. Anderson, a veteran teacher of 15 years, stood at the front of her classroom, trying to summon the enthusiasm she used to carry effortlessly. On this Monday, however, her usually vibrant voice wavered. She had spent the previous week grading papers, analyzing data from the quarterly benchmark exams, attending a school district training, and juggling her family's needs. Exhausted, she tried to encourage her students, but her words felt hollow—even to her. By lunch, her frustration boiled over. "How am I supposed to give my best when there's nothing left of me to give?" she whispered to a colleague, her eyes heavy with unshed tears. This was more than burnout—it was "Empty Cup Syndrome," when emotional and mental depletion make even the kindest intentions feel like a burden.

Mrs. Anderson's repeated exposure to stress is rewiring her brain's neural pathways. The circuits that once fired easily for joy, patience, and motivation are weakening from underuse, while the pathways tied to frustration, fatigue, and survival mode are becoming stronger and more automatic. Over time, this shift makes it harder for her brain to access the calm, creative responses she once relied on—and easier to feel overwhelmed, defeated, or emotionally drained, even in familiar situations.

Mrs. Anderson's story resonates because it's not just hers—it's the story of countless professionals who find themselves pouring into others when their own cup is dangerously low. Educators, caregivers, healthcare workers, business leaders, and even parents often push themselves beyond their limits, believing that sacrifice is the hallmark of commitment. But what happens when the sacrifice comes at the cost of their own well-being? Empty Cup Syndrome creeps in silently, convincing us that running on fumes is noble, when in reality, it's unsustainable. Without intentional refilling, those who are called to give the most risk losing the very things that makes their presence powerful: their voice, their passion, and their purpose.

The truth is this: You cannot pour inspiration, motivation, or belief into your students if your own reservoir is dry. The most powerful words lose their power when they come from an empty place. Eleanor Brownn once said, "You can't serve from an empty vessel. Take care of yourself first so that you can give your best to the ones who need you most." This chapter, along with Chapter 8, "The Overflow Principle", is written with love and for the purpose of refilling and rewiring.

Teacher Rewired

The first base on the Classroom DNA strand is **Teacher: Self**—and for good reason. It is the most essential, most catalytic base of all. It doesn't just sit at the start; it activates the entire sequence. Without it, the strand doesn't fire. Without it, the classroom doesn't come alive. Every transformation, every spark of engagement, every shift in culture begins not with a strategy, but with you.

But here's the truth that few talk about: before you can ignite a passion for learning in your students, you must first ignite it within yourself. Before you can speak belief into a child who's given up, you must learn to speak life into the person in front of the mirror. This is where neuroplasticity enters the scene—not as a scientific term to admire, but as a personal tool for transformation.

Neuroplasticity is the brain's remarkable ability to rewire itself based on repeated thoughts, behaviors, and spoken words. The story you tell yourself—daily, subconsciously, habitually—becomes the architecture your brain builds upon. Every time you say, "I can't," a neural pathway is reinforced. Every time you say, "I was made for this," a new pathway is formed. Your words don't just leave your lips—they leave a footprint in your brain. And over time, that footprint becomes a highway.

That's why the words you choose matter—your thoughts, words, and actions will naturally follow the most frequently traveled routes in your brain. The goal is to intentionally create and strengthen positive, healthy neuropathways—so that encouragement, confidence, and resilience become your brain's default setting.

So, when we talk about recoding classroom DNA, we're not just talking about techniques or lesson plans. We're talking about the deep, neurological reprogramming that begins with a teacher's internal dialogue. What you believe about yourself becomes the energy your students feel. What you say to yourself becomes the standard for what your students say to themselves. It is your inner language that sets the tone, the atmosphere, and the temperature of your classroom.

You see, your life—and your classroom—will always follow the direction of your most dominant thoughts and your most repeated words. Speak survival, and you'll feel stuck. Speak growth, and your brain will begin to wire for possibility. Neuroplasticity doesn't ask for perfection; it responds to consistency. So, if you want to change the narrative of your classroom, you must first rewrite the narrative in your own mind.

This year, your greatest teaching tool isn't on a curriculum map. It's not a strategy in a binder. It's your voice. Start using it on yourself.

Voice-Activate:

Developing the habit and culture of speaking life-producing phrases into one's own life is foundational to a teacher's ability to pour positivity into their students. Here's how a teacher can connect the very first base on the Classroom DNA strand:

1. Reflect on Personal Mindset

- ▶ **Step:** Identify and challenge negative self-talk patterns.
- ▶ **Purpose:** Awareness of negative thoughts is the first step toward replacing them with life-producing words.
- ▶ **Action:** The words you choose first thing in the morning can influence not only your mindset but also the energy you bring into your classroom. By starting your day with empowering language, you create a ripple effect that can inspire both you and your students to approach challenges with confidence and optimism. Instead of saying, "Ugh, it's going to be a rough day," try saying, "This is going to be a great day. I am blessed. I am strong. I am capable." By doing this, you're activating your day for success. Remember, the way you speak in the morning shapes the reality you will experience throughout the day.

2. Set Daily Life-Producing Phrases

- ▶ **Step:** Start the day with life-producing phrases that align with your goals and values.
- ▶ **Purpose:** Positive statements reinforce confidence and focus for the day ahead.
- ▶ **Action:** Write phrases such as:

  - ✓ I am valued and respected for the work I do in shaping young minds.
  - ✓ Wisdom, patience, and creativity rest upon me today.
  - ✓ The students on my roster are making strides in learning each day.
  - ✓ I trust my intuition and creativity to find solutions in difficult situations.
  - ✓ I am a great teacher, and I teach great students.
  - ✓ I am continuously learning and evolving as a teacher.
  - ✓ I bring joy and enthusiasm into my classroom, making learning exciting.
  - ✓ I am making a lasting difference in the lives of my students.
  - ✓ I am confident in my ability to inspire and motivate my students.
  - ✓ I am proud of the progress my students and I make together.
  - ✓ I am deserving of rest and self-care, which enhance my teaching.

3. Develop a Prayer and Worship Practice

- ▶ **Step:** Start or deepen a daily prayer and worship routine.
- ▶ **Purpose:** Aligning with God's truth and seeking His guidance fills your heart with life-giving words.
- ▶ **Action:**

✓ Begin each day in prayer, asking for strength, wisdom, and the ability to speak life into yourself and others.

✓ Read Scriptures or devotionals that emphasize the power of words (e.g., Proverbs 18:21: "The tongue has the power of life and death.")

✓ Incorporate worship music that uplifts and encourages, creating an atmosphere of peace and positivity.

4. Create a Positive Environment

▶ **Step:** Surround yourself with uplifting influences.

▶ **Purpose:** The environment you are in can impact your mindset and self-talk.

▶ **Action:**

✓ Limit time with negative or draining individuals.

✓ Display inspirational quotes or Scriptures in your workspace.

✓ Choose music, books, or podcasts that encourage growth and positivity.

5. Reframe Challenges as Opportunities

▶ **Step:** Change the way you speak about difficulties.

▶ **Purpose:** Reframing fosters a growth mindset and builds resilience.

▶ **Action:** When faced with challenges, replace "This is too hard" with "This is an opportunity to grow and learn something new." Too often, we use words thoughtlessly, unaware of the impact they have. Phrases like, "These students are too far behind," or "My students will never understand this new math," or "It's always going to be this way," reinforce negative beliefs and create an environment where those outcomes can flourish. When you speak negatively, you're essentially laying the foundation for a path you don't want to follow. Yet, it becomes the path you'll walk because of what you've constructed with your words. Now, consider the opposite: when you choose to speak words of empowerment and victory, you're paving a different path entirely.

6. Practice Gratitude Daily

▶ **Step:** Reflect on what you're thankful for.

▶ **Purpose:** Gratitude shifts focus from shortcomings to abundance and blessings.

▶ **Action:** Write down three things you're grateful for each day, such as supportive colleagues, a moment of clarity, or progress with a student. End your list with a simple prayer of thanks, like, "Lord, I thank You for every blessing, big and small, in my life."

7. Acknowledge Your Wins

▶ **Step:** Celebrate small and big achievements.

▶ **Purpose:** Recognizing success builds confidence and reinforces the habit of self-encouragement.

▶ **Action:** At the end of each day, say, "Today I accomplished..." and name at least one thing you're proud of.

8. Speak Life in the Mirror

▶ **Step:** Verbally activate yourself each day.

▶ **Purpose:** Hearing positive words about yourself rewires your brain for confidence.

▶ **Action:** Stand in front of a mirror and say phrases like, "I am a positive force in my classroom," and "I have what it takes to succeed."

9. Be Kind to Yourself in Mistakes

▶ **Step:** Replace self-criticism with compassion.

▶ **Purpose:** Self-compassion fosters resilience and reduces stress.

▶ **Action:** When you make a mistake, say, "I'm human, and this is part of learning. Next time, I'll approach it differently." Pray for patience and wisdom, saying, "Lord, help me grow through this moment and trust in Your grace."

10. Visualize Your Best Self

▶ **Step:** Picture yourself thriving in your personal and professional life.

▶ **Purpose:** Envisioning success inspires belief and positive actions.

▶ **Action:** Take five minutes daily to close your eyes and visualize your ideal day—how you will feel, speak, and accomplish your goals. Follow this by praying, "Lord, guide me to live out this vision with Your strength."

11. Develop a "Replenishment Plan"

▶ **Step:** Intentionally refill your emotional and mental "cup."

▶ **Purpose:** Speaking life into yourself is easier when you feel replenished and cared for.

▶ **Action:** Create a list of activities that bring you joy and peace, such as:

✓ Getting a massage
✓ Taking a weekend vacation
✓ Taking a walk in nature
✓ Meditating or practicing mindfulness
✓ Engaging in hobbies or spending time with loved ones
✓ Spending quiet time in prayer or reading the Bible

12. Practice Consistency and Patience

▶ **Step:** Commit to speaking life into yourself daily.

▶ **Purpose:** Building a habit of positivity takes time and dedication.

▶ **Action:** Set a reminder on your phone or calendar to pause during the day and repeat a life-giving phrase. Track your progress in a gratitude or voice-activating phrases journal. End your day with a prayer of reflection, asking God for continued guidance and strength.

The positive words you release into the atmosphere about yourself become the foundation upon which the recoding process of your classroom's DNA begins. This first conduit, "Teacher to Him/Herself," is the most vital base and cannot by any means be overlooked. If you have been searching for a surefire way to create a culture-rich classroom that is conducive to teaching and learning, you will experience results with your thoughts, words, and beliefs.

Now, it's your turn. Write down three life-producing phrases that you will speak at the start of each day:

1._____

2._____

3._____

When you speak life into yourself, you'll be more equipped to pour positivity, encouragement, and hope into the lives of those you teach, creating a ripple effect that extends far beyond your classroom.

T H E   2 N D
B A S E   P A I R

Teacher : Atmosphere

VOICE - ACTIVATED CLASSROOM FRAMEWORK

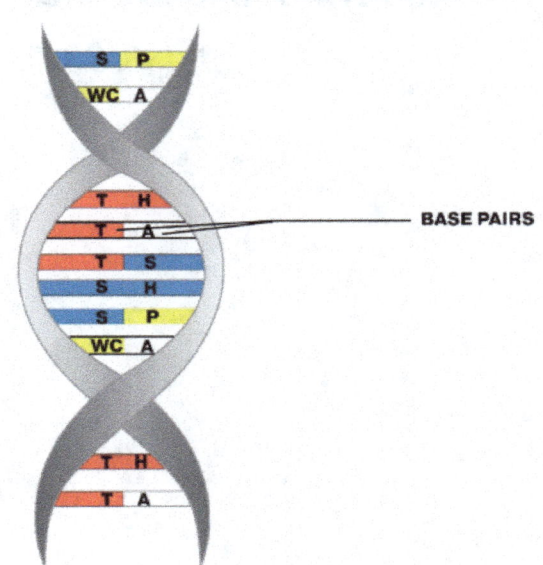

T = TEACHER
S = STUDENTS
P = PEERS / WC - WHOLE CLASS
A = ATMOSPHERE
H = HIM / HERSELF

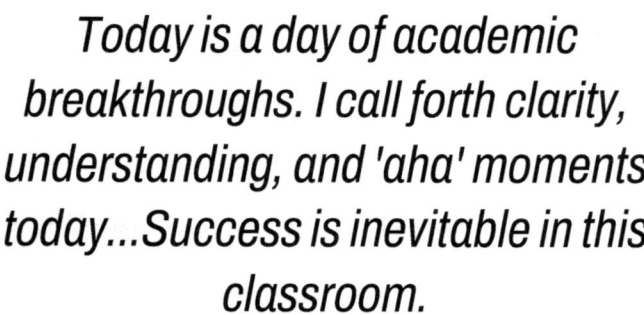

Today is a day of academic breakthroughs. I call forth clarity, understanding, and 'aha' moments today...Success is inevitable in this classroom.

CHAPTER 2

PROGRAM THE ATMOSPHERE

Teacher: Atmosphere

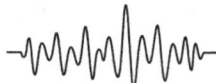

T he room listens.

Even empty chairs absorb the energy of your voice.

Imagine walking into your classroom early in the morning—the air still, the chairs empty, the hush of anticipation resting gently in the room. This moment, often overlooked, holds sacred potential. It's not just a pause before the chaos of the day; it's a chance to set the emotional thermostat of your classroom before a single student walks through the door. When you speak positive, life-producing words into the atmosphere, you're not just filling space—you're shaping it.

Speaking into the atmosphere is an intentional act of creation. Your words carry vibrational energy, subtle yet powerful enough to influence the emotional tone, the learning climate, and even the neural pathways forming in your students' brains. What you say before the day begins can become the blueprint for how the day unfolds.

This is the second base on the Classroom DNA strand: **Teacher: Atmosphere**. And it is here that you learn one of the greatest truths of teaching—your voice doesn't just teach, it transforms the air your students breathe.

As a former classroom teacher and school principal, I have witnessed firsthand the powerful effects of speaking life-producing words and phrases into my classrooms and on the campuses where I served. As a teacher, I arrived in my classroom around the same time that the head custodian arrived to open the school building. Early mornings were the best time for me to set the tone for my day and to activate the second base of the Voice-Activated Classroom DNA Structure. Mornings are the best time to recode a classroom's DNA. As I turned on the lights, I simultaneously turned on my voice to begin activating my classroom before the students arrived. I spoke directly to the atmosphere because I knew that it could hear me.

I would say, "Good morning, classroom. You are a haven for learning, respect, and collaboration. Distractions and negativity will not reside here. Every student who enters this classroom is destined for success. Success, higher-order thinking, and confidence flow freely here today. Today is a day of academic breakthroughs. I call forth clarity, understanding, and 'aha' moments today. This room is alive with purpose and potential. Success is inevitable in this classroom. Today will be a blessed day."

During my career as a teacher and campus leader, I have taught and led students at private, parochial, and public schools. Most of my career was spent on Title I campuses. A classroom's DNA can be recoded on any type of school campus, no matter the ethnicity, race, socioeconomic background, or academic level of the students. Life-producing words, mixed with a little belief, are the key elements to a successful recoding.

Now, was everyday a perfect day in my classrooms or on my school campuses? Absolutely not! There were many challenging days. But, when I began to implement Base 1 and Base 2 of the Voice-Activated Framework, I responded to challenges through a different set of lenses, with a different mindset, and with better solutions.

As teachers, we often focus on the words we say directly to our students, but the atmosphere we create with our words before they even arrive can be just as impactful. Our words have the power to mold the very air that students breathe.

Voice-Activate:

Before the start of the school year, classrooms can be likened to a void space. The world was once void before it was transformed into a realm of fullness and abundance, brimming with life and possibility, all through the simple act of speech. Your classroom is brimming with life and possibilities, so let's get to speaking.

1. Understand the Power of Atmosphere

▶ **Step:** Recognize that a teacher's words and energy shape the environment before students enter.

▶ **Purpose:** A teacher's spoken words can set the tone for a day of peace, focus, and positivity in the classroom.

▶ **Action:**

✓ Reflect on the belief that your words create a foundation for learning and growth.

✓ Acknowledge that speaking life into the atmosphere prepares the space for success, just like preparing lesson plans or organizing materials.

2. Pray or Reflect Over the Classroom

▶ **Step:** Begin each morning with prayer or quiet reflection in the classroom.

▶ **Purpose:** Inviting peace, wisdom, and positivity into the space helps establish a foundation for the day.

▶ **Action:**

✓ Pray, "Lord, bless this classroom. Let it be a space of learning, respect, and growth for every student who enters."

✓ Reflect on the impact you want to make: "Today, I speak life into this room. It will be a place of joy, safety, and progress."

3. Walk the Classroom and Speak Life Aloud

▶ **Step:** Physically move through the room while speaking positive declarations into the space.

▶ **Purpose:** Your voice and presence activate the atmosphere, infusing it with encouragement and intention.

▶ **Action:**

✓ As you walk, speak voice-activating phrases aloud:

- "Atmosphere! Get ready! You will soon be filled with eager students who are ready to learn, students who are not afraid to tap into the great potential inside of them."
- "This is a place where students feel valued and respected."
- "Learning is exciting and meaningful in this room."
- "Every student who enters this space is capable of success."

4. Set the Tone for Specific Areas

▶ **Step:** Speak life over specific zones in the classroom (e.g., desks, group areas, materials).

▶ **Purpose:** Tailored voice-activating phrases create an atmosphere of purpose and positivity for every activity.

▶ **Action:**

✓ At the students' desks: "These desks are places of focus and achievement."

✓ At the group table: "This table is a space for collaboration and teamwork."

✓ Near materials: "These tools will inspire creativity and understanding."

5. Write and Display Life-Producing Phrases

▶ **Step:** Place visual reminders of positivity throughout the classroom.

▶ **Purpose:** Written voice-activating phrases reinforce the energy you've spoken into the room.

▶ **Action:**

✓ Display voice-activating phrases like:

   • "This is a space of kindness and growth."

✓ "Mistakes are part of learning."

✓ "We are a team, and we support one another."

✓ Write new voice-activating phrases for the start of each week or month to keep the energy fresh.

6. Dedicate the Start of the Year to Atmosphere Building

▶ **Step:** Speak life into the classroom while setting it up before the school year begins.

▶ **Purpose:** Establishing the atmosphere early creates a strong foundation for the year.

▶ **Action:**

✓ A few days before the students return to the classroom is the perfect time to activate classrooms across the world with words. Maximize this time to speak life into the empty classroom space. Announce to the atmosphere statements such as:

- "Empty space, I speak life into you! This is a space where learning barriers are dismantled and where comprehension skills improve at a steady pace."

✓ As you arrange furniture or hang posters, say:

- "This room will be a sanctuary of learning and joy."
- "Every student who enters this classroom will feel seen, heard, and supported."
- "This will be a year of growth, breakthroughs, and success."

✓ Play uplifting music or instrumental tracks while working to maintain a peaceful and joyful atmosphere.

7. Use Music or Sound to Enhance the Atmosphere

▶ **Step:** Play soft, uplifting music or nature sounds as part of your morning ritual.

▶ **Purpose:** Music can amplify your words and fill the room with calm, positive energy.

▶ **Action:**

✓ Select instrumental tracks, calming sounds or positive music.
✓ As the music plays, walk the room and say, "This is a space where everyone thrives."

8. Visualize the Day Ahead

▶ **Step:** Picture the students entering the room and thriving in the space you've prepared.

▶ **Purpose:** Visualization helps align your words with a clear and hopeful vision for the day.

▶ **Action:**

✓ Close your eyes and imagine students arriving, excited, focused, and ready to learn.

✓ Speak aloud, "Today will be a day of connection, discovery, and progress."

9. Speak to the Future

▶ **Step:** Declare positive outcomes for the day, week, and year.

▶ **Purpose:** Speaking life into the future sets expectations for long-term success and growth.

▶ **Action:**

✓ Say: "This classroom will be a place where every student grows academically and emotionally."

✓ Repeat: "This year, students will overcome challenges and exceed expectations."

10. Dedicate Time Daily Before Students Arrive

▶ **Step:** Make speaking life into the classroom a daily habit.

▶ **Purpose:** By speaking life into the atmosphere before students arrive, the teacher ensures that the classroom is a welcoming, peaceful, and empowering space. This intentional practice not only prepares the room for learning but also positions the teacher as a source of stability and inspiration for the day ahead.

▶ **Action:**

✓ Arrive early enough to have quiet time in the room.

✓ Speak voice-activating phrases aloud while walking, tidying, or preparing for the day.

✓ Commit to this practice, even if only for a few minutes, to center yourself and the space.

✓ NOTE: Do not fret if the school year is already in full swing; this action can be taken anytime the classroom is empty. Lunch breaks, planning periods, before the school day begins, and at the end of the school day are all great moments to serve as the conduit between your voice and the atmosphere.

11. Monitor and Reflect on the Atmosphere

▶ **Step:** Pay attention to how your words influence the classroom environment over time.

▶ **Purpose:** Reflection helps you adjust and maintain a positive atmosphere.

▶ **Action:**

✓ At the end of the week, ask yourself:

- "How did the classroom feel this week?"
- "Did I notice any changes in the students' energy or focus?"

✓ Adjust your morning life-producing phrases as needed to align with classroom needs.

Now, it's your turn. Write down three life-producing phrases that you will speak into your classroom atmosphere before your students arrive:

1._____

2._____

3._____

T H E   3 R D
B A S E   P A I R

Teacher : Students

VOICE - ACTIVATED CLASSROOM FRAMEWORK

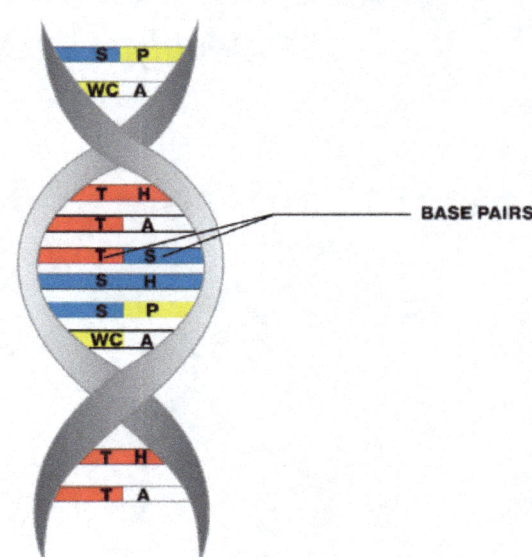

T = TEACHER
S = STUDENTS
P = PEERS / WC - WHOLE CLASS
A = ATMOSPHERE
H = HIM / HERSELF

BASE PAIRS

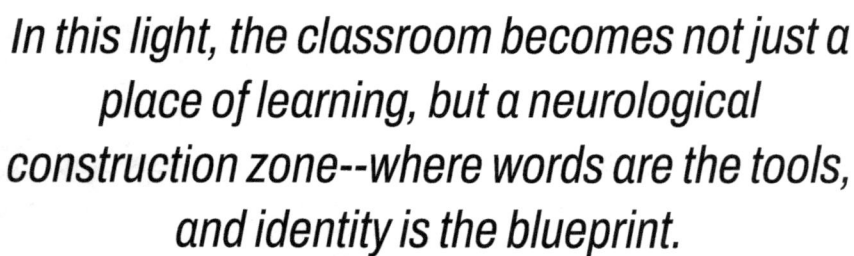

In this light, the classroom becomes not just a place of learning, but a neurological construction zone--where words are the tools, and identity is the blueprint.

CHAPTER 3

TRANSFER THE POWER

Teacher: Students

-ﻭﻭﻭﻭﻭﻭﻭﻭ-

C odes, not compliments.
The spoken word becomes cellular instruction—recoding identities and igniting academic belief.

Ms. Mays

In the early 1990s, as a young student teacher, I interned in a first-grade classroom with a teacher named Ms. Mays at a high-poverty public school. There were over 20 students in the class, comprised of mostly African American students and a handful of ESS (English as a Second Language) students from various countries. Every morning, Ms. Mays began her class with a declaration: "You are brilliant. You are problem-solvers. You are kind. You are unstoppable." She believed in the transformative power of words and spoke life into her students daily. From the start, she made eye contact with each child, ensuring they felt the sincerity behind her life-producing words.

Throughout the day, Ms. Mays reinforced her words with actions. If a student struggled with a math problem, she'd kneel beside them and say, "You are a critical thinker. Let's work on this together." When mistakes happened, she reassured them, "You are resilient. Mistakes are steps toward success."

Andre was a shy student who rarely participated, until one day he raised his hand. Ms. Mays smiled and said, "Andre, you are courageous. Thank you for sharing." From that moment, his confidence grew, and he began engaging more often. The students soon mirrored her phrases, encouraging each other with phrases like, "You've got this!"

Ms. Mays didn't offer compliments for the sake of kindness—she spoke with surgical precision, using affirming words to *recode* how her students saw themselves. Every "You are" statement was intentional, designed not to flatter but to *rewire* neural pathways that had been shaped by doubt, struggle, or silence.

Neuroscience confirms what she instinctively practiced: repeated positive statements activate the brain's prefrontal cortex, the region responsible for decision-making, self-perception, and goal-setting. Over time, these forward-thinking phrases create new, stronger neural connections that help students internalize confidence as part of their identity—not just as encouragement, but as truth.

Transfer The Power

The third base of the Voice-Activated Classroom DNA Strand, **Teacher: Students** was now connected. Ms. Mays' natural release of positive, life-producing words into the lives of her students created an environment where growth and empowerment lived. By the year's end, her students had not only achieved academic success but also developed strong self-worth.

Don't get this confused with mere positive reinforcement. What Ms. Mays was doing—and what research now affirms—is intentional *recoding* of the brain's neural pathways through the daily use of forward-thinking, life-producing phrases. This isn't about praise for performance; it's about speaking directly to identity. An article in the *Journal of Psychologists and Counsellors in Schools* explains that when teachers consistently deliver positive statements, students experience measurable gains in self-esteem, self-talk, and self-efficacy. But the power lies deeper than the surface—it's neurological. Each time a student hears, "You are capable," or "You are a critical thinker," the brain responds by strengthening the synaptic connections associated with that belief. The more often these phrases are repeated and internalized, the more dominant those pathways become— reshaping not only how a student sees themselves, but how their brain is wired to believe, behave, and become. In this light, the classroom becomes not just a place of learning, but a neurological construction zone—where words are the tools, and identity is the blueprint.

As educators, the words we speak to our students carry a profound ability to breathe life into their spirits, activating something deep within them that drives their growth and success. When we choose to speak life-producing words, we aren't just offering encouragement—we are unlocking potential, sparking confidence, and connecting the third base of the classroom DNA strand together.

Speaking life into the lives of students involves directly informing and affirming their abilities, potential, and value. Teachers can use words that recognize students' efforts, encourage them in their struggles, and celebrate their achievements. This approach is rooted in the belief that words can shape identity, self-esteem, and beliefs about one's capabilities.

VOICE-ACTIVATE:

To begin recoding your classroom's DNA by speaking life-producing phrases into students and developing a habit and culture of speaking life, take the following steps:

1. Reflect on Personal Beliefs

- ▶ **Step:** Examine your own beliefs about teaching and your students' potential.
- ▶ **Purpose:** You cannot speak life into others if you don't believe in their ability to succeed. Ensure your mindset aligns with the belief that every student has the potential to grow.
- ▶ **Action:** Journal about your "why" for teaching and remind yourself of your calling to positively influence students.

2. Set an Intention Daily

- ▶ **Step:** Begin each day with a clear intention to uplift and encourage.
- ▶ **Purpose:** A focused intention helps align words and actions throughout the day.
- ▶ **Action:** Use voice-activating phrases like, "Today, I will encourage my students to see their strengths and believe in themselves."

3. Create a Repository of Life-Producing Phrases

- ▶ **Step:** Prepare a list of positive and empowering phrases to use regularly.
- ▶ **Purpose:** Having a bank of voice-activating phrases ensures that you are prepared to speak life even in challenging moments.
- ▶ **Action:** Examples include:
  - ✓ "I believe in you."
  - ✓ "You are capable of amazing things."
  - ✓ "Mistakes are part of learning and growing."

4. Incorporate Positive Talk into Classroom Routines

- ▶ **Step:** Make positive language a structured part of the day.
- ▶ **Purpose:** Consistency fosters a habit and culture of positivity.
- ▶ **Action:**

  - ✓ Begin each day with a class voice-activating phrases.
  - ✓ End lessons by acknowledging effort and growth (e.g., "You all worked hard today, and I see your progress!").
  - ✓ Use encouraging transitions like, "Let's approach this new challenge as an opportunity to shine."

5. Model Positive Self-Talk

- ▶ **Step:** Demonstrate how to reframe negativity into positivity.
- ▶ **Purpose:** Students learn how to speak life by watching their teacher model it.
- ▶ **Action:** When faced with challenges, say aloud, "This is tough, but I know I can figure it out."

6. Encourage Students to Speak Life

- ▶ **Step:** Teach students to speak life-producing words to themselves and their peers.
- ▶ **Purpose:** A culture of positivity emerges when students actively contribute to it.
- ▶ **Action:**

  - ✓ Assign a daily "voice-activating phrase leader" to share an uplifting phrase with the class.
  - ✓ Teach students to uplift their peers during group activities.

7. Be Intentional in Difficult Moments

▶ **Step:** Choose words carefully during conflicts or disappointments.

▶ **Purpose:** Even corrective feedback can uplift when phrased positively.

▶ **Action:** Replace, "You're not trying hard enough," with, "I know you're capable of more, and I'm here to help you get there."

8. Celebrate Growth and Achievements

▶ **Step:** Acknowledge students' efforts and successes regularly.

▶ **Purpose:** Voice-Activating phrases solidify the power of life-giving words.

▶ **Action:** Use phrases like, "Look at how far you've come!" or "I'm so proud of the way you tackled that problem."

9. Envision the Classroom You Want

▶ **Step:** Picture the outcomes of a positive classroom environment.

▶ **Purpose:** Envisioning success sets a powerful tone for your words and actions.

▶ **Action:** Write down how you want students to feel and perform, then create short, actionable phrases that align with your vision.

10. Be Consistent and Patient

▶ **Step:** Practice speaking life daily, even when results aren't immediate.

▶ **Purpose:** Creating habits and culture take time and persistence.

▶ **Action:** Set small goals for daily positive interactions, and track your progress.

By following these steps, you are connecting the third base of the Classroom DNA Strand, while transforming your classroom environment into a space where positivity and encouragement thrive, fostering students' confidence and growth.

Now, it's your turn. Write down three life-giving phrases that you will speak into your students' lives:

1._____

2._____

3._____

THE 4TH
BASE PAIR

Student : Him/Herself

VOICE - ACTIVATED CLASSROOM FRAMEWORK

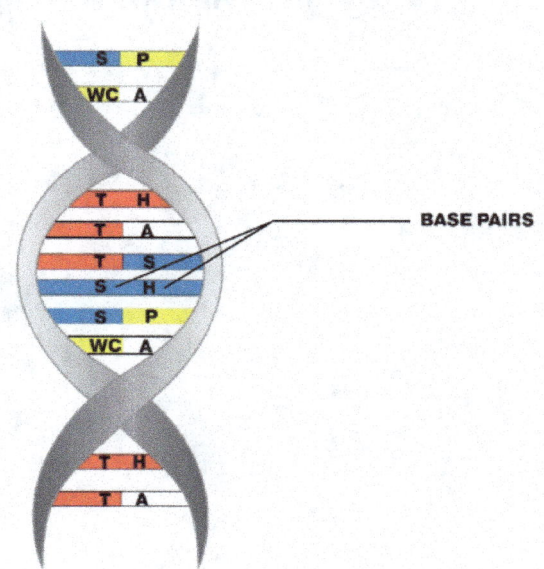

T = TEACHER
S = STUDENTS
P = PEERS / WC - WHOLE CLASS
A = ATMOSPHERE
H = HIM / HERSELF

BASE PAIRS

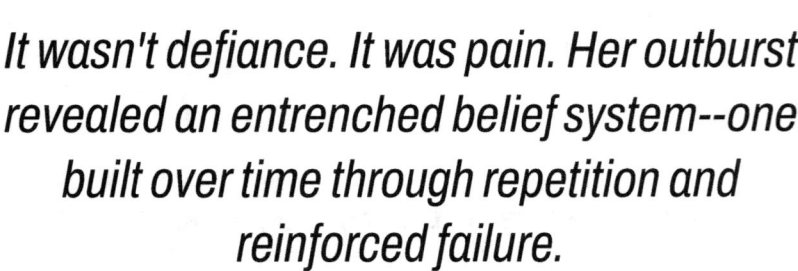

It wasn't defiance. It was pain. Her outburst revealed an entrenched belief system--one built over time through repetition and reinforced failure.

CHAPTER 4
DISMANTLE SELF-SABATOGE

Student: Him/Herself

T alk trains thoughts.

The beliefs students build in silence become the lives they live in public.

Bridgett

When I began teaching third grade in Atlanta, Georgia, I was blessed with a student named "Bridgett"—a social butterfly with a short attention span, seemingly allergic to her seat, and academically struggling. By lunchtime on any given day, Bridgett had been redirected at least 25 times. Despite her redirections, Bridgett had a radiant smile, a bubbly spirit, and a sense of humor that lit up the room. But none of those traits could substitute the fact that Bridgett didn't believe in her own brilliance.

One afternoon, I sat with her on the steps at recess. She opened up about not having help at home—her family had recently immigrated, and they were busy starting a business. She often felt alone. That conversation shifted everything. Her behavior wasn't about defiance. It was about unmet needs, unspoken fears, and a nervous system wired for survival instead of focus.

That afternoon, after the classroom emptied, I stood by Bridgett's desk and began to speak aloud: *"Bridgett will become less impulsive. She will grow more attentive. She will believe in herself. I am grateful that I was chosen to be her teacher."* I was activating the atmosphere—because I knew words weren't just sound. They were codes. They were signals. And in the right environment, they would rewire her brain.

Rewiring the Routine

I created a simple plan: I placed two index cards and a kitchen timer on Bridgett's desk. One card had words from me: *"You've got this." "I believe in you."* The other card was blank, waiting for Bridgett's voice. She began writing her own "I AM" statements, like *"I am focused"* and *"I am learning."* These were more than positive phrases—they were activators, rewiring her inner dialogue.

The timer helped her practice staying seated for short bursts. Each success earned her a tally mark, a moment of celebration, and a dose of dopamine, reinforcing her new behavior. By the end of the week, she was graphing her own progress, sharing updates with her parents, and becoming a student who took ownership of her growth.

This wasn't just behavior management. It was brain transformation. According to neuroscientists Andrew Newberg and Mark Robert Waldman, *"A single word has the power to influence the expression of genes that regulate physical and emotional stress."* In other words, our words change the wiring of the brain—literally.

The Outburst—and the Turning Point

One afternoon, the students received their test results to bring home. I heard papers crash to the floor. Then came Bridgett's shout:

"I never get good grades!"

It wasn't defiance. It was pain. Her outburst revealed an entrenched belief system—one built over time through repetition and reinforced failure. Her voice echoed a fixed mindset carved deep into her neural pathways.

Instead of yelling or reacting, I wrote a note: *"I believe in you. After you pick the papers up, let's talk about a plan to improve your grades."*

That moment became our pivot point. I started meeting with Bridgett on Saturday mornings for one-on-one tutoring. (Yes, I used an hour or so of my personal time and invested it in Bridgett.) Each session began with life-giving words: *"You are smart. You're getting better every day."* Then we tackled content and study habits, rewiring not just how she thought, but how she learned.

According to Newberg and Waldman, *"If you repetitively focus on positive words and images, anxiety and depression will decrease, and the number of negative thoughts will decline."* Bridgett was living proof.

Voice-Activation in Action

Bridgett began to repeat her new truth aloud: *"I'm getting better at this every day!"*

Peer support followed. When she met a goal, the class celebrated. Her progress became a shared victory. That's the power of student-to-peer voice-activations—another pillar of the Voice-Activated Classroom. Positive social language increases oxytocin levels and builds emotional safety, which the brain *needs* in order to learn. Eventually, Bridgett was named "Student of the Week," earned both the "Most Improved" and "Academic Growth" awards, and transformed into the young scholar she once thought she couldn't be.

Bridgett's story is a living case study of how words—spoken by the teacher, by the student, by peers, and into the atmosphere—can change brains. Her journey is proof that when we speak life, we activate growth. When we shift language, we shift learning. And when we choose our words with intention, we become brain-changers, not just behavior managers.

What happened in Bridgett's mind was not magic. It was neuroplasticity. It was science. It was voice-activation in motion.

Dismantle Self-Sabotage

"Sticks and stones may break my bones, but words will never hurt me." It's a chant many of us learned in childhood, intended as armor against hurtful words. But as we grow older, we learn the truth: words do hurt. Especially the ones we silently repeat to ourselves. For students, the internal echo of negative comments—whether from peers, adults, or past failures—can form a soundtrack of self-sabotage. "I'm not smart enough." "I always mess things up." "Why even try?" These self-inflicted wounds don't just linger—they imprint.

This is where neuroplasticity becomes a powerful ally. The brain is not fixed, it's flexible. It reshapes and rewires itself based on repeated thoughts, patterns, and beliefs. When students constantly replay harmful phrases, their brains begin to hardwire those negative pathways, reinforcing feelings of inadequacy and hopelessness. But here's the good news: those same pathways can be rewired. When students replace negative self-talk with voice-activating, empowering language, they begin to dismantle the stronghold of self-sabotage and build new neural circuits rooted in confidence, resilience, and possibility.

That's why the fourth step in the Voice-Activated Framework, **Student: Him/Herself**, focuses on the relationship between the students and themselves. Teachers play a vital role in helping students recognize the power of the words they speak internally. By intentionally teaching students how to choose words that showcase their worth and potential, educators activate a shift—not just in speech, but in brain structure and self-belief. A student who learns to say, "I am capable," "I can learn this," or "I am enough," begins the work of rebuilding their inner world.

When students are taught to speak life to themselves, they don't just change their mindset—they transform their biology. They become living proof that words can rewire the brain and recode the heart. And when that shift happens, the classroom evolves into a space where students don't just survive—they thrive.

VOICE-ACTIVATE:

To connect the fourth base of the Classroom DNA strand, teachers must teach students how to speak life-producing words into their own lives. It is important to guide students through the following series of practices to help them understand the impact of their words and how to use language positively.

1. Introduce the Power of Words

- ▶ **Step:** Teach students about the impact of words on their mindsets and emotions.
- ▶ **Purpose:** Students need to understand that their words can shape their beliefs and actions.
- ▶ **Action:**

    - ✓ Begin with a simple exercise: ask students to write down how they feel when they hear positive versus negative words.
    - ✓ Share examples of how words can build confidence or tear it down (e.g., "I can do this!" versus "I'm terrible at this!").
    - ✓ Use visuals, such as a diagram of the brain's response to positive self-talk.

2. Set the Tone with Class Life-Producing Phrases

▶ **Step:** Incorporate daily class-wide life-producing phrases to model positive self-talk.

▶ **Purpose:** Creating a shared practice normalizes speaking life and sets an example for students to follow.

▶ **Action:**

    ✓ Begin each day with phrases like, "I am capable of learning new things," or "I bring value to this classroom."

    ✓ Encourage students to say them aloud together to build confidence and camaraderie.

3. Teach the Science Behind Self-Talk

▶ **Step:** Explain how positive and negative words affect the brain and emotions.

▶ **Purpose:** Students are more likely to embrace self-talk when they understand its physiological and psychological effects.

▶ **Action:**

    ✓ Show how positive words strengthen neural pathways, improving resilience and focus.

    ✓ Use age-appropriate visuals or videos to demonstrate concepts like neural plasticity and the "power of yet."

4. Guide Students in Creating Personal Life-Producing Phrases

▶ **Step:** Help students write their own life-producing phrases.

▶ **Purpose:** Personalized life-producing phrases are more meaningful and impactful.

▶ **Action:**

    ✓ Provide sentence starters like "I am," "I can," and "I will."

✓ Encourage students to reflect on their strengths, goals, and aspirations while creating life-producing phrases.

- "I am an excellent student. I excel at my daily objectives."
- "I am capable of learning and mastering new concepts."
- "I have the strength to overcome any challenges that come my way."
- "I can handle peer pressure with confidence and poise."
- "I will comprehend, retain, and apply new learning today."
- "My efforts lead to success, and I believe in my abilities."
- "Every mistake is an opportunity for growth and improvement."
- "I am focused, attentive, and eager to learn."
- "There is greatness inside of me."
- "I am resilient and can bounce back from setbacks stronger than before."
- "I trust in my ability to solve problems and think critically."

5. Reinforce Positive Self-Talk During Challenges

▶ **Step:** Model and encourage positive self-talk when students face difficulties.

▶ **Purpose:** Challenging moments are critical opportunities for students to practice speaking life.

▶ **Action:**

✓ When a student struggles, guide them to replace negative thoughts with phrases like, "I can figure this out," or "Mistakes are how I learn."

✓ Celebrate small victories, saying, "Look at what you've already achieved!"

6. Incorporate Gratitude Practices

▶ **Step:** Teach students to focus on what they are thankful for.

▶ **Purpose:** Gratitude helps shift attention from negativity to positivity, creating fertile ground for speaking life.

▶ **Action:**

   ✓ Use a "gratitude journal" in which students write three things they are thankful for daily.

   ✓ Pair gratitude with life-producing phrases, such as "I'm grateful for my effort today; I know I'm improving."

7. Create a "Speak Life" Culture

▶ **Step:** Embed positive language into classroom interactions and routines.

▶ **Purpose:** A positive environment helps students adopt and sustain habits of speaking life.

▶ **Action:**

   ✓ Create a "compliment wall" where students can write encouraging notes to each other.

   ✓ Reward students who use positive self-talk or encourage peers.

8. Practice Role-Playing

▶ **Step:** Use role-playing to practice responding to real-life situations with positive self-talk.

▶ **Purpose:** Practicing scenarios helps students internalize and apply what they've learned.

▶ **Action:**

✓ Present a situation like failing a test or struggling with a project, and ask students to role-play positive responses.

✓ Provide phrases like, "I didn't do well this time, but I'll ask for help and do better next time."

9. Provide Visual Reminders

▶ **Step:** Use posters, charts, and bulletin boards to reinforce positive self-talk.

▶ **Purpose:** Visual cues help students stay mindful of speaking life to themselves.

▶ **Action:**

✓ Create a class voice-activation poster with students' contributions.

✓ Display quotes or images that inspire positivity, such as "I believe in me!"

10. Celebrate Progress

▶ **Step:** Acknowledge when students use positive self-talk and encourage them to keep it up.

▶ **Purpose:** Celebrating reinforces habits and motivates students to continue.

▶ **Action:**

✓ Use statements like, "I noticed you encouraged yourself during that math problem—great job!"

✓ Share weekly reflections where students write or share how speaking life has helped them.

11. Model Speaking Life Daily

▶ **Step:** Be a consistent example of positive self-talk.

▶ **Purpose:** Students will imitate what they observe from you.

▶ **Action:**

✓ Verbally reframe your own challenges in front of the class (e.g., "This is a tough lesson to teach, but I'm excited to figure out how we'll get through it together!").

✓ Speak life into students with phrases like, "I see so much potential in you," and "You are making great progress."

12. Reflect as a Class

▶ **Step:** End the week with a class reflection on the power of words.

▶ **Purpose:** Reflection deepens understanding and reinforces learning.

▶ **Action:** Ask students to share:

✓ An example of a time when they spoke life to themselves.

✓ How it made them feel.

✓ How they will continue using positive self-talk next week.

By following these steps, a teacher can cultivate a classroom culture in which students not only learn how to speak life to themselves but also begin to believe in their unique potential and capacity for growth. This habit will not only create a growth culture in your classroom, but it can also transform students' outlooks on challenges and improve their confidence for years to come.

Now, it's your turn. Write down three life-producing phrases that you would like to have your students speak or phrases they have chosen themselves:

1._____

2._____

3._____

THE 5TH BASE PAIR

Student : Peers

VOICE - ACTIVATED CLASSROOM FRAMEWORK

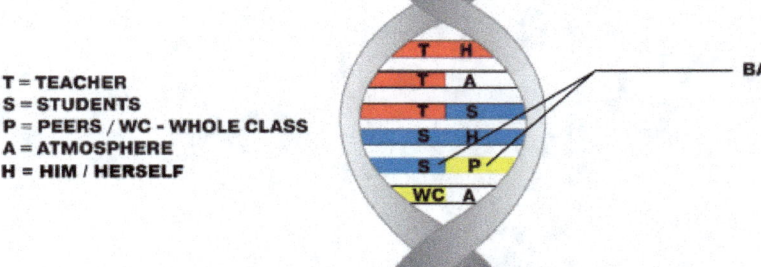

T = TEACHER
S = STUDENTS
P = PEERS / WC - WHOLE CLASS
A = ATMOSPHERE
H = HIM / HERSELF

BASE PAIRS

Students who received consistent peer support reported a 40% decrease in stress levels and showed significantly higher resilience and motivation to tackle academic challenges.

CHAPTER 5

NORMALIZE PEER ACTIVATIONS

Student: Peers

Peers plant patterns.

The brain remembers peer praise more deeply than corrections—it stores them as emotional blueprints.

The Quiet Kid

He was quiet most days. Sat near the back, rarely raised his hand. Many teachers might not have noticed him—but on this day, he did something unexpected. After a peer struggled through reading a passage aloud, stumbling over every third word, this quiet boy leaned over and whispered just loud enough for his friend to hear:

"You did good, bro. Keep going."

And in that small moment—no applause, no intervention, no grade—it happened.

Growth.

Not the kind you can measure with a rubric or standard. The kind that happens when someone feels seen, feels supported, and feels safe. That is the magic of a peer's voice in activating classroom DNA. And that is why what students say to each other is just as powerful as what we say to them.

Normalize Peer Activations

In a world filled with noise, pressure, and negativity, one of the most important things we can teach students is how to empower each other through connection. Base Five of the Voice-Activated Classroom DNA Strand, **Student: Peers**, focuses on the words students speak to one another. The way they interact with their classmates shapes the heart of the classroom culture.

When students learn to speak life into their peers, they're doing more than being kind—they're building bridges. Bridges over troubled waters. For many students, the classroom may be the only stable and recoding environment they experience. A kind word from a peer can be the difference between emotional isolation and feeling seen. In today's world, in which students navigate anxiety, social pressure, identity struggles, and often traumatic experiences, peer-to-peer support becomes a lifeline. These bridges of connection help students carry heavy loads they may never speak aloud, creating spaces of safety and shared humanity.

By using uplifting, supportive, and life-producing language, students create a web of encouragement that uplifts everyone in the room. This peer-to-peer connection cultivates kindness, mutual respect, and a collective sense of belonging.

Research on child development confirms that encouragement from peers reduces anxiety and stress while also strengthening a growth mindset. In fact, a study published in the Journal of Youth and Adolescence found that students who received consistent peer support reported a 40% decrease in stress levels and showed significantly higher resilience and motivation to tackle academic challenges. Challenges begin to feel like steppingstones instead of stumbling blocks. When life-producing words come from a classmate, they often land with even more power, boosting confidence, increasing participation, and sparking collaboration.

Empowering students to speak with intention to their peers activates a culture of shared success—where every voice matters, and every student feels seen, supported, and capable of greatness.

VOICE-ACTIVATE:

To cultivate a classroom culture where students actively encourage one another, begin by implementing the following steps:

1. Connect Speaking Life to Themselves with Speaking Life to Others

- ▶ **Step:** Help students understand that speaking life to others starts with the positivity they've already cultivated in themselves.
- ▶ **Purpose:** Reinforce the connection between self-voice-activation and peer encouragement to show how both practices strengthen relationships.
- ▶ **Action:**

  - ✓ Facilitate a discussion: "How has speaking life to yourself helped you? How might it feel to share that encouragement with others?"
  - ✓ Share examples of how voice-activating others can build confidence, trust, and a supportive classroom culture.

2. Introduce the Benefits of Speaking Life to Peers

- ▶ **Step:** Teach students how speaking life to others creates positive ripple effects.
- ▶ **Purpose:** Students are more likely to practice peer encouragement when they understand its impact.

▶ **Action:**

✓ Share benefits such as:

- Building stronger friendships
- Boosting others' confidence
- Creating a happier, more supportive classroom environment

✓ Use real-life stories or examples (e.g., how teamwork improves when peers encourage each other).

3. Model Peer Encouragement

▶ **Step:** Demonstrate specific ways to speak life to others.

▶ **Purpose:** Students need clear examples of how to transition from internal activations to activating their peers.

▶ **Action:**

✓ Share phrases like, "I appreciate the way you helped me," or "You're really great at explaining things."

✓ Model these phrases in real time during group activities or class discussions: "Thank you, Ella, for sharing your idea— that was thoughtful."

4. Practice Peer-to-Peer Life-Producing Phrases

▶ **Step:** Create structured opportunities for students to practice speaking life to their peers.

▶ **Purpose:** Practice builds confidence and normalizes encouraging language in peer interactions.

▶ **Action:**

✓ Use activities like "Partner Compliments," where students pair up and share one specific thing they admire about their partner.

✓ Conduct a "Peer Spotlight," where each student receives encouragement from classmates about their strengths or accomplishments.

5. Create a Peer Encouragement Challenge

▶ **Step:** Encourage students to actively seek moments to speak life to their peers throughout the day.

▶ **Purpose:** A challenge makes the practice intentional and helps build long-term habits.

▶ **Action:**

✓ Launch a "Kindness Tracker," where students record times when they've encouraged others or received encouragement themselves.

✓ Recognize class milestones, like "100 Peer Compliments," with celebrations or rewards.

6. Discuss Empathy and Intentionality

▶ **Step:** Teach students the importance of being thoughtful and genuine in their words.

▶ **Purpose:** Speaking life is most impactful when rooted in empathy and authenticity.

▶ **Action:**

✓ Discuss questions like, "How do we know what someone needs to hear?" and "How can we make sure our words come from the heart?"

✓ Role-play scenarios where students practice responding to a peer's struggle with life-producing and supportive language.

7. Embed Peer Encouragement in Daily Routines

▶ **Step:** Integrate peer encouragement into existing class routines.

▶ **Purpose:** Daily practice helps students make peer activations a natural part of their interactions.

▶ **Action:**

> ✓ Start each day with a "Morning Shout-Out," where students can acknowledge something kind or impressive a peer did.
>
> ✓ End the week with "Positive Peer Fridays," where students write notes of encouragement to classmates.

8. Incorporate Group Activities with Positive Reinforcement

▶ **Step:** Use collaborative projects to promote peer encouragement.

▶ **Purpose:** Working together provides natural opportunities to practice speaking life.

▶ **Action:**

> ✓ Assign group roles like "Encourager" to ensure that someone is responsible for cheering on their teammates.
>
> ✓ Debrief after group work by asking, "How did encouraging each other help us succeed?"

9. Celebrate Peer Encouragement in Action

▶ **Step:** Highlight examples of students speaking life to their peers.

▶ **Purpose:** Public recognition reinforces positive behaviors and inspires others to follow suit.

▶ **Action:**

✓ Share specific moments during class meetings: "I noticed that Jayden told Mia her idea was really creative during group work—that's what speaking life looks like!"

✓ Create a "Words That Shine" bulletin board where students can post notes of appreciation for their classmates.

10. Introduce Reflection and Gratitude Practices

▶ **Step:** Encourage students to reflect on how speaking life to peers impacts their relationships and the classroom environment.

▶ **Purpose:** Reflection deepens awareness of the positive effects of encouragement.

▶ **Action:**

✓ Ask students to journal or discuss: "How did it feel to encourage a peer today? How did they respond?"

✓ Pair reflections with gratitude by having students identify one kind thing a peer said to them during the week.

11. Teach Conflict Resolution with Speaking Life

▶ **Step:** Show students how to use life-producing phrases even during disagreements.

▶ **Purpose:** Peer encouragement isn't just for positive moments; it can also de-escalate conflict and rebuild trust.

▶ **Action:**

✓ Role-play scenarios in which students use life-producing language during conflicts (e.g., "I appreciate your perspective, and here's how I feel.")

✓ Reinforce phrases like, "Let's figure this out together," or "I respect you, and I want us to work this out."

- ## 12. Reflect as a Class

▶ **Step:** Regularly evaluate how peer encouragement is shaping the classroom.

▶ **Purpose:** Reflection ensures that students see the progress and value of speaking life to their peers.

▶ **Action:**

✓ Hold monthly discussions: "How has encouraging each other changed how we feel in class?"

✓ Use reflective prompts like, "What's one thing a peer said to you that made your day better?"

By focusing on these steps, a teacher can deepen students' understanding of how to speak life to their peers and foster a culture of kindness, empathy, and support in the classroom, all while creating healthy neuropaths in the brain. This approach helps students see the mutual benefits of uplifting each other, creating a positive ripple effect that extends beyond the classroom walls.

Implementing these strategies includes students in the process of creating an environment in which life-producing words are a natural and integral part of the classroom culture. By being intentional and consistent, teachers can help students realize the power of their words to shape both their own and others' lives.

This environment type reduces competition and comparison, replacing them with a sense of shared growth and collective success. It also helps students develop social-emotional skills, including active listening, giving and receiving positive feedback, and building healthy relationships.

As students experience activations from their peers, they become more likely to develop a positive self-concept and a sense of belonging, which are critical for academic and personal growth.

Now, it's your turn. Write down three life-producing phrases that students can say to their peers in your classroom:

1._____

2._____

3._____

THE 6TH BASE PAIR

Whole Class : Atmosphere

VOICE - ACTIVATED CLASSROOM FRAMEWORK

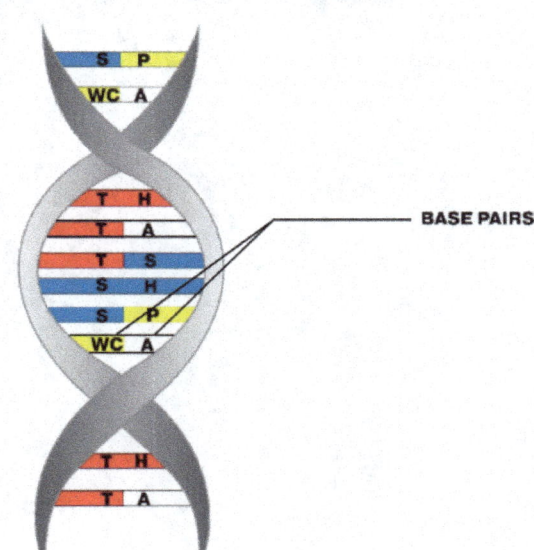

T = TEACHER
S = STUDENTS
P = PEERS / WC - WHOLE CLASS
A = ATMOSPHERE
H = HIM / HERSELF

BASE PAIRS

Positive environments don't just make students feel better--they make their brains work better by reinforcing the formation of healthy, lasting neural pathways.

CHAPTER 6

RECALIBRATE THE ATMOSPHERE

Whole Class: Atmosphere

E nvironments echo euphony.

The moment every student speaks life aloud, the classroom begins to breathe differently, and the DNA of learning is rewritten on the spot.

There is Power in Unity

You're not just changing one student; you are changing the classroom. So, when you change the words spoken into the classroom, you change the way students speak to themselves. And when students change the words they speak to each other, that's when the classroom rewires itself.

The sixth and final base of the *Classroom DNA Framework* is perhaps the most electrifying of all: **Whole Class: Atmosphere**. This base ignites when the entire classroom comes together to speak life-producing words into the air they share. It is not only a morning ritual but an atmospheric recalibration. A collective declaration that the space will be one of respect, focus, and boundless potential.

When every student lifts their voice in unity—activating, coding, believing—their words don't just echo through the room; they charge it. Energy rises. Tension dissolves. The atmosphere shifts. Just as nature responds to sound and vibration, the classroom responds to the frequency of agreement. When the whole class speaks in one accord, it creates a sound...a harmonious combination of words that serves as a threat to negativity.

According to Immordino-Yang and Damasio (2007), positive emotional and social environments in the classroom are essential for optimal brain function. When students feel safe, connected, and encouraged, the brain releases dopamine and oxytocin—chemicals that increase motivation, enhance memory, and strengthen neuroplasticity. In other words, positive environments don't just make students feel better—they make their brains work better by reinforcing the formation of healthy, lasting neural pathways

Starting each class period with this unified voice doesn't just set the tone—it rewires it. A tone that cultivates dignity, belonging, and excellence isn't accidental; it's neurological. Every time students speak life together, they activate the brain's reward pathways, reinforce positive neural circuits, and prime the mind for deeper learning. And because the brain thrives on repetition, this collective practice doesn't fade when the bell rings—it echoes in their mindset, memory, and motivation. When one voice becomes many, the atmosphere doesn't just come alive—it becomes neurologically aligned for growth.

VOICE-ACTIVATE:

The final base of the Classroom DNA Strand is Base 6: Whole Class to the Atmosphere. Follow the steps below to complete the voice-activation framework.

1. Introduce the Concept of Speaking Life into the Atmosphere

▶ **Step:** Explain how words spoken collectively can influence the classroom environment and outcomes.

▶ **Purpose:** Students need to understand that their combined voices can create a powerful, unified impact.

▶ **Action:**

✓ Share an analogy, such as this one comparing the classroom to a symphony: "Each instrument plays a role, but when they all come together, they create something extraordinary. Our words can work the same way."

✓ Use examples like cheering for a team or singing together, illustrating how group words can uplift and inspire.

2. Teach the Power of Agreement

▶ **Step:** Introduce the concept that unity in speaking positive words amplifies their effect.

▶ **Purpose:** Help students understand that speaking life as a class aligns their focus and energy toward shared goals.

▶ **Action:**

✓ Share a simple phrase like, "When we all believe and speak the same positive words, we create an atmosphere of success and encouragement."

✓ Use an example, such as agreeing as a group to say, "We are a team, and we help each other succeed."

3. Model Speaking Life into the Atmosphere

▶ **Step:** Demonstrate how to speak life into the atmosphere as a teacher, and involve the students.

▶ **Purpose:** Students need a clear example of how this practice looks and feels.

▶ **Action:**

    ✓ Start class by saying, "Today is going to be a great day of learning and growing. Let's speak that together."

    ✓ Invite the students to repeat the phrase together, emphasizing energy and belief in their words.

4. Create Shared Life-Producing Phrases

▶ **Step:** Guide the class in developing a group activation to speak daily.

▶ **Purpose:** A shared life-producing phrase fosters unity and gives students ownership of the atmosphere they create.

▶ **Action:**

    ✓ Collaboratively write positive phrases for the whole class to speak into the atmosphere, such as:

- "Together, we can achieve great things!"
- "We are a team, and we support each other."
- "Our classroom is a place of respect and learning."
- "We are capable of reaching our reading/math goals."
- "Every one of us adds value to our class."
- "We will face challenges with determination and teamwork."
- "Our combined efforts will lead to success."
- "We believe in our ability to excel."
- "We are committed to creating a positive learning environment."
- "Our unity makes us stronger and more successful."
- Post it visibly in the classroom, and recite it together each morning.

5. Practice Speaking Life for Specific Goals

▶ **Step:** Use speaking life into the atmosphere to focus on shared goals or challenges.

▶ **Purpose:** Applying this practice to real situations reinforces its power and purpose.

▶ **Action:**

✓ Before a test or project, lead the class in saying, "We are prepared, confident, and capable of doing our best."

✓ Afterward, reflect together: "How did speaking life help us feel and perform today?"

6. Use Collective Voice-Activating Phrases to Set the Tone

▶ **Step:** Begin and end each day or class period with voice-activating phrases as a group.

▶ **Purpose:** Consistency in speaking life helps students internalize the practice and sets a positive tone for learning.

▶ **Action:**

✓ Start the day with, "Today we will learn, grow, and support each other."

✓ End the day with, "We had a productive day, and we are proud of our efforts."

7. Incorporate Physical Gestures for Emphasis

▶ **Step:** Pair phrases with movements or gestures to make them more impactful.

▶ **Purpose:** Physical actions help students engage more fully and solidify the energy of their words.

▶ **Action:**

✓ Use gestures like raising hands when saying, "We rise to every challenge!"

✓ Create a "power pose" that the class adopts while speaking their phrases.

8. Encourage Responsibility for the Classroom Atmosphere

▶ **Step:** Empower students to use their words to maintain a positive environment.

▶ **Purpose:** Students need to see their role in creating and sustaining a positive atmosphere.

▶ **Action:**

✓ Discuss how words like "We can do this" uplift the class, while words like "This is boring" bring it down.

✓ Encourage students to call out positive phrases during group activities or challenges.

9. Use Reflection to Reinforce the Power of Agreement

▶ **Step:** Reflect with students on how speaking life into the atmosphere has impacted the class.

▶ **Purpose:** Reflection helps students recognize and appreciate the effects of their collective words.

▶ **Action:**

✓ Ask questions like, "How did our words help us focus and feel confident today?"

✓ Encourage students to share examples of how speaking life has influenced their learning or mood.

10. Extend Speaking Life to Broader Goals

▶ **Step:** Teach students to use their collective voice to speak life into goals beyond the classroom.

▶ **Purpose:** Show students how this practice can apply to life, teamwork, and community.

▶ **Action:**

✓ Lead Life-Producing like, "We will make a difference in our school and community," or "We are a team that supports and uplifts each other."

✓ Encourage students to use this practice in sports teams, clubs, or at home.

11. Celebrate Milestones Together

▶ **Step:** Acknowledge successes that come from speaking life as a class.

▶ **Purpose:** Celebrating reinforces the power of agreement and motivates continued practice.

▶ **Action:**

✓ Host a "Speak Life Celebration" when the class achieves a shared goal, such as completing a project or improving behavior.

✓ Highlight specific moments when speaking life positively influenced the classroom atmosphere.

By teaching students the power of agreement and guiding them to speak life into the atmosphere, you empower them to shape their environment with intention and positivity. This practice not only transforms the classroom but also equips students with a life skill they can carry into every aspect of their future.

Now, it's your turn. Write down three life-changing phrases that your whole class can speak into the atmosphere:

1._____

2._____

3._____

Conclusion of Part I

When the six (6) base pairs of the Voice-Activated Classroom DNA Model—speaking into the atmosphere, speaking life into students' lives, and having students speak life to each other—are connected and consistently practiced, they create a powerful synergy that transforms the classroom climate:

▶ **Reinforces Positive Beliefs:** When a classroom is filled with brain-activating and positive words, students start to believe that positive outcomes are possible and even likely, shifting from a mindset focused on limitations to one focused on opportunities. Positive language becomes a constant reinforcement of growth, potential, and worth. This creates a self-reinforcing cycle in which students' beliefs about themselves and their capabilities continually grow stronger.

▶ **Builds a Supportive Culture:** A classroom culture where positivity is spoken into the atmosphere and reinforced by both teachers and peers builds a safe and supportive community. This reduces anxiety and stress, allowing students to focus better, engage more deeply, and take on challenges without fear of failure or judgment.

▶ **Encourages Accountability and Ownership:** When students are encouraged to speak life into each other, they take ownership of the classroom environment. They learn that their words have power and responsibility, and they begin to hold themselves and each other accountable for maintaining a positive and respectful atmosphere.

Part II

THE
GENETIC
CODE

T
T/A
T/S
S/H
S/P
WC/A

T
T/A
T/S
S/H
S/P
WC/A

T
T/A
T/S
S/H
S/P
WC/A

*"The human brain is not a courtroom where guilt or intelligence is decided.It's a **genetic code** being written in real-time.Every word spoken to a student is like a gene being switched on or off—either activating confidence, curiosity, and resilience or triggering doubt, fear, and disengagement."*

-Dr. LaKesa (TEDxJesterCirED, 2025)

CHAPTER 7

AWAKEN THE UNMOTIVATED

One year, I was blessed with a student I'll call Sam.

Sam was physically present but mentally absent—slouched in his chair, hoodie pulled low, eyes fixed on his desk. He had mastered the art of invisibility. Every classroom before mine had labeled him: lazy, careless, inattentive. And when a student hears those words often enough, they begin to wear them like a second skin. They don't just believe the labels—they become them.

But here's the deeper truth: disengagement is rarely about disinterest. Often, it's about self-preservation. Sam wasn't choosing to opt out of learning. He was shielding himself from the pain of trying and failing yet again. He had learned that detachment was safer than disappointment.

To reach him, I knew I couldn't demand participation or coax him into caring. I had to go deeper. I had to rewrite the internal script—the words Sam believed about himself. So I began speaking to him differently. I would say, "Sam, I see how you sit back, watching. You're not disengaged, you're observant. And that means you have something important to say."

At first, he shrugged, dismissing my words. But the brain listens to repetition, especially when it contradicts years of negative conditioning.

The more I spoke those words over him, the harder they became to ignore. Slowly, something began to shift.

But what truly made the difference wasn't just my voice—it was the voices of his peers. I taught my students how to speak life into each other. We practiced shifting our language from criticism to coding, from sarcasm to support. They began to say things like, "Man, you're smart. Why you acting like you don't know this? Give it a try." It wasn't fake encouragement—it was peer-to-peer truth-telling, rooted in belief. And that shift? That was the breakthrough. Because sometimes, a student won't believe the teacher, but they'll believe the kid sitting next to them.

One day, during a lively class discussion, I looked at Sam and asked, "What's your take on this?" There was a pause, and for the first time, there was no shrug. No silence. Sam spoke. He added his thoughts. His voice entered the room, and the room made space for it.

That was a win!

But the win wasn't just in that one moment. The real win was the culture we had built—a classroom where coding through uplifting language was expected, and every student understood the power they held in their words. A culture where speaking life into others became the norm, not the exception.

It started with intentional language, spoken by me to my students and modeled by my students to each other. That was how we unlocked Sam's potential. And that's how we can unlock the potential of countless others: by turning classrooms into cultures of belief, one word at a time.

Too often, teachers misread the signs. A blank stare is mistaken for disrespect. A refusal to turn in work is labeled laziness. A slouched posture becomes a reason to call home or send the student out of class. But what if those behaviors aren't rebellion—but a response? What if that child isn't resisting your instruction but retreating from their own internal storm?

Disengaged students are often navigating invisible battles—poverty, trauma, anxiety, grief, instability, or chronic academic failure. Their brain, quite literally, is wired for survival, not learning. According to neuroscientist Dr. Bruce Perry, when a student is in a state of persistent stress, their brain remains in the lower "survival" regions, namely the brainstem and midbrain. These parts govern fear, safety, and fight-or-flight responses. The prefrontal cortex, where logic, focus, planning, and motivation reside, is offline. The unmotivated student isn't choosing apathy—they're neurologically trapped in it.

In his work on neurosequential development, Dr. Perry explains: "You can't teach a kid who isn't regulated. You must reach the brain in the right order: regulate, relate, reason." This sequence is essential. You don't awaken motivation with a worksheet or a warning. You do it with connection, compassion, and consistency.

Let's be clear: motivation isn't something you extract from a student. It's something you ignite. And thanks to the power of neuroplasticity—the brain's ability to reorganize itself by forming new neural connections—we know that even students who've been stuck in patterns of withdrawal or failure can relearn how to engage, try, and succeed. But first, they must believe that effort is safe and that their teacher sees more than their behavior—they see the human beneath it.

Practical Steps to Awaken the Unmotivated

1. Regulate Before You Educate

A dysregulated student cannot engage in meaningful learning. Begin each day or class period with a simple grounding activity: deep breathing, a calming prompt, music, or a positive activation phrase. These small, intentional practices help shift the brain out of survival mode and begin to rewire a sense of safety and routine.

Try This Tomorrow:

Before the bell rings, say: "Take a deep breath in. Let it out. You are safe here. You belong here. You can do hard things."

2. Reframe the Narrative

Instead of asking, *"Why won't this student try?"* ask, *"What obstacle is standing in the way of this student's effort?"* This reframing helps you move from frustration to curiosity, and curiosity is the birthplace of connection.

3. Speak Life Through Strategic Praise

Neuroscientific research shows that positive reinforcement creates dopamine surges, which stimulate motivation and memory. But praise must be specific, authentic, and effort-focused to activate the brain's reward system. Instead of saying "Good job," say:

"I saw how you kept going even when the assignment got hard. That's grit. That's growth."

Over time, these statements build new neural pathways that associate effort with reward and belonging.

4. Use the Power of Predictability

Students from chaotic environments often live in a state of hypervigilance. Predictable routines and consistent teacher responses calm the amygdala and create space for engagement. A structured environment isn't strict— it's safe. And safety is a prerequisite for motivation.

5. Create Opportunities for Voice and Choice

Motivation flourishes when students feel agency. Give even your most withdrawn student small choices:

"Do you want to start with question one or five?"
"Want to explain this out loud or write your answer?"

Agency awakens ownership. Ownership builds engagement.

6. Tell Them Who They Are Becoming

Neuroplasticity thrives on repetition and belief. Speak into their potential. Say it often. Say it like you mean it.

"I see a future leader in you."

"You're becoming someone who doesn't give up."

"You haven't quit yet—that says a lot about your character."

When students begin to internalize these messages, their brains start rewiring themselves toward growth rather than defense.

Let's return to the student in the hoodie. The one who hasn't lifted his head in days. You could walk past him. Or you could whisper,

"I know things have been hard, but I haven't given up on you."

You could write him a sticky note that says,

"I'm still rooting for you."

You could choose to believe that inside him, there is a spark—not dead, just dormant. And with the right words, the right tone, and the right presence, you just might be the match that awakens it.

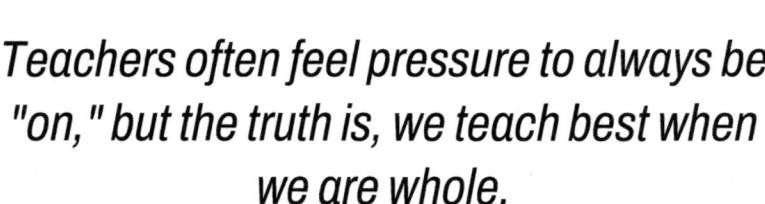

Teachers often feel pressure to always be "on," but the truth is, we teach best when we are whole.

CHAPTER 8
THE OVERFLOW PRINCIPLE

T o best serve others, we must operate from a place of abundance. Imagine a pitcher of water. When the pitcher is full, it pours easily, nourishing everything around it. When it's halfway full, it struggles to meet demands. And when it's empty, tilting it only produces a dry, grating sound. The pitcher is not broken; it simply needs refilling. This is the essence of the overflow principle: you cannot pour effectively into others unless your own needs are met first. Positive, life-producing words are part of that overflow—when our hearts and minds are filled with peace, gratitude, and activation, our words naturally reflect that abundance. They build up, restore, and energize. But when we operate from a place of tension, exhaustion, or frustration, our words become strained, sharp, and disconnected. Instead of pouring life, we unknowingly deplete the atmosphere around us. The flow of impact always begins within. If the source is dry, the stream is too.

Operating from overflow means giving from your abundance rather than your reserves. It requires intentional practices to ensure that your mental, emotional, and physical health remain robust enough to meet life's demands. A study published in the *Journal of Occupational Health Psychology* reinforces this idea, showing that individuals who prioritize self-care and maintain personal well-being are more effective in their roles, both professionally and personally. Teachers and administrators experiencing burnout often struggle with lower patience levels, reduced creativity, and diminished empathy, all of which directly affect student outcomes. A teacher who is energized and fulfilled brings warmth, patience, and optimism into the classroom, transforming the learning environment.

The overflow principle is deeply tied to energy transfer—and if you're an educator, you've felt it. Emotional energy is not static; it moves, transfers, and multiplies. Some days, you walk into your classroom feeling strong, centered, and focused. Your students can feel it too. Other days, when you're running on empty, they feel that as well. But it's important to remember that your words are not just energy—they're a lifeline. In moments when you feel drained, stressed, or even hopeless, the right words—spoken aloud or silently to yourself—can shift your inner atmosphere. Words like "I can handle this," "This moment won't last forever," or "I'm still making a difference" may seem small, but they hold power.

Neuroscience tells us that through neuroplasticity, the brain is constantly forming and strengthening neural pathways based on repetition. Every time you choose life-producing words over defeatist thoughts, you're rewiring your brain—building pathways that restore energy, build resilience, and sustain you through hard days. This is why it's vital to speak words that fuel your future, not just describe your frustration. The more often you choose words of strength, hope, and clarity, the more automatic those thoughts become. They serve as an inner reserve of energy, especially when your outer world feels depleted. Choosing your words wisely isn't just about positivity—it's about survival, sustainability, and overflow.

Teacher Testimony – Mrs. White, Fourth-Grade Teacher

"I remember one day I sat in my car before school, completely overwhelmed. I was behind on grading, I had a parent conference I was dreading, and I hadn't slept much the night before. I almost cried right there in the parking lot. But instead, I said out loud, 'You were chosen for this. You have what it takes.' I repeated it all the way to my classroom. I didn't feel better right away—but I felt stronger. And every time I repeated those words, I noticed my shoulders drop a little, my breath slow down, and my mind begin to clear. That moment taught me that my words are more than positive thinking—they are tools that carry me through. Now, I keep a sticky note on my desk that says: 'Your words are your reset.'"

The overflow principle also emphasizes prevention. You don't have to wait until you're empty to refill your cup. Proactively maintaining your well-being creates a buffer, ensuring that the inevitable stresses of life do not deplete you entirely. In practical terms, this might mean setting boundaries to protect your time, investing in activities that bring you joy, or simply allowing yourself moments of stillness amid a busy day. These small but consistent actions create a wellspring of energy that sustains not only you but also those who rely on your support.

The Side Effects of Pouring from an Empty Cup

Pouring from an empty cup has consequences far beyond the individual. Emotional fatigue sets in, making meaningful connections with students challenging. Physical health declines, leading to increased absenteeism and diminished classroom presence. Cognitive functions, like decision-making and creativity, suffer. Relationships—with students, colleagues, and even family—become strained.

The ripple effect is most evident within the classroom. Students are remarkably perceptive and can sense when their teacher is overwhelmed or disengaged. Take the case of Ms. Alvarez, an elementary teacher who loved incorporating music and storytelling into her lessons. After a particularly grueling semester filled with administrative demands and personal challenges, she stopped singing and storytelling altogether. Her students, once lively and eager, grew restless and distracted. It wasn't until Ms. Alvarez took a weekend retreat to recharge that she realized how much her depleted energy had influenced her students. When she returned, reinvigorated, the atmosphere in her classroom shifted dramatically. "When I took care of myself, I saw my students light up again," she shared.

The connection between teacher well-being and student success is well documented. Studies have shown that teacher burnout correlates with lower student achievement and higher behavioral issues. Neuroscientific research supports this as well: a stressed teacher's brain operates from survival mode, limiting access to higher-order thinking and problem-solving skills. This state not only affects the teacher's performance but also the classroom's emotional climate. Students thrive in environments where they feel supported and valued, and this starts with a teacher who can model emotional regulation and positivity.

In a middle school in Chicago, a mindfulness program for teachers yielded remarkable results. Teachers who practiced mindfulness reported lower stress levels and greater job satisfaction. Their classrooms became more harmonious, with students reporting feeling safer and more understood. "It's like the teacher's calm became our calm," one student remarked. The overflow principle was at work: as teachers replenished their own cups, they poured into their students with greater patience, empathy, and creativity.

The Ripple Effect of Overflow

Operating from abundance allows you to serve not just as a teacher or leader but as a source of inspiration. A teacher who models balance and self-care teaches students a vital life lesson: taking care of yourself is not a sign of weakness but a foundation for strength. Mrs. Anderson, after realizing her exhaustion was affecting her classroom, began delegating tasks, prioritizing sleep, and rediscovering her passion for gardening. Within weeks, her classroom transformed. "My students became more engaged, and I had more energy to give them," she said. "It was like I got my spark back."

When you pour from a place of overflow, your energy, enthusiasm, and care become contagious. Students respond to a teacher who is fully present, creating a classroom culture of mutual respect and vitality. The overflow principle reminds us that to give our best to others, we must first give our best to ourselves.

The phrase "fill me up till I overflow" is a figurative expression that captures the essence of living and giving from a place of abundance. It reflects a desire to be so filled with positivity, joy, or purpose that spills over and impacts others. The imagery of an overflowing cup signifies not just sufficiency but abundance—a state in which needs are met, and there is more to share.

So How Do We Refill Our Cup When We Feel Empty?

It begins with permission—granting ourselves the right to rest, reflect, and recharge without guilt. Teachers often feel pressure to always be "on," but the truth is, we teach best when we are whole. Here are a few intentional strategies to combat *Empty Cup Syndrome* and restore the energy needed to speak life into others:

1. **Schedule Non-Negotiable "Me Time"** – Even 15 minutes a day of quiet, reflection, or doing something you love can begin to fill your emotional reservoir.

2. **Create Boundaries and Stick to Them** – Saying "no" to yet another committee or volunteer request isn't selfish—it's self-preservation.

3. **Limit Exposure to Negative Energy** – Spend less time around draining conversations, toxic breakroom talk, or people who always focus on what's wrong.

4. **Practice Daily Life-Producing** – Speak life over yourself first. Try beginning each morning with simple statements like "I am enough," "I am making a difference," or "I give myself permission to rest."

5. **Connect with Life-Giving Colleagues** – Find your tribe. Sometimes, just one uplifting conversation with a fellow educator can reignite your spark.

6. **Do Something That Has Nothing to Do with School** – Hobbies, laughter, movement, or moments of creativity can reset your mindset in powerful ways.

7. **Check In with Your Body** – Are you sleeping enough? Drinking water? Moving? The physical self is often the first to warn us when our cup is running low.

8. **Seek Support Without Shame** – Talking to a therapist, coach, or trusted mentor can provide clarity and compassion in times of stress.

9. **Celebrate Small Wins** – Even on your toughest day, something went right. Train your brain to notice it.

10. **Speak Kindly to Yourself** – Your internal dialogue matters. If you wouldn't say it to your students, don't say it to yourself.

Your capacity to serve others is only as strong as your commitment to serving yourself. The truth about pouring is simple: an empty cup serves no one. As you navigate the demands of your profession and life, remember that filling your cup is not an indulgence; it's an investment. Choose to operate from abundance, and watch how the lives you touch are transformed—including your own.

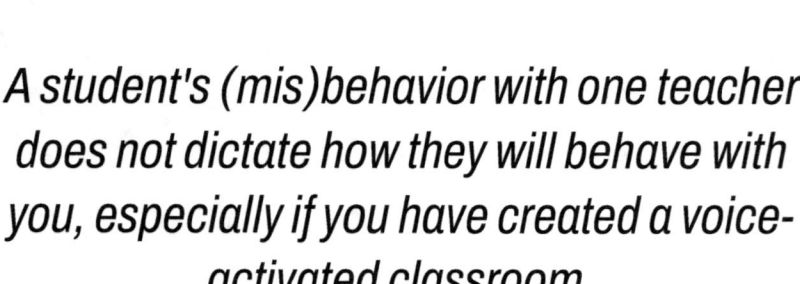

A student's (mis)behavior with one teacher does not dictate how they will behave with you, especially if you have created a voice-activated classroom.

CHAPTER 9
SPEAK, BELIEVE, ACHIEVE

The true magic unfolds when a teacher combines faith and belief with action, particularly the unwavering conviction that every child is destined for success. This belief resonates with the words of Maya Angelou, who famously said, "I've learned that people will forget what you said, people will forget what you did, but people will never forget how you made them feel." When teachers embody this principle, they create an environment where every student feels valued and capable, setting the stage for transformative learning experiences.

When educators genuinely believe that each child can succeed, they are inspired to take meaningful actions that reflect this faith. This may involve developing personalized learning strategies, providing additional support while covering challenging topics, or simply taking the time to connect with students on a personal level by making activating statements such as "You can do this. I believe in you." Such actions not only demonstrate a teacher's commitment, but they also communicate to students that they are worthy of attention and investment.

A teacher's belief in a student's potential must be non-biased, extending beyond factors such as skin color, gender, academic performance, or appearance. This belief is a powerful, impartial force that acknowledges the worth and capability of every student, regardless of whether they wear the same uniform all week or struggle academically. When a teacher holds an unbiased belief in each student's potential, they foster an inclusive environment where all students are seen as capable of success. By removing preconceived notions or judgments and consistently communicating this belief through words, actions, and attitudes, the teacher demonstrates a true commitment to equity. This non-biased belief empowers students to rise above their challenges and internalize their teacher's confidence in them. It nurtures a sense of self-worth, motivating students to see themselves as capable of achieving their goals, regardless of the obstacles they face.

Social psychology research reveals that when individuals feel believed in, it significantly impacts their behavior and performance. This belief acts as a powerful motivator, encouraging individuals to take on challenges they might otherwise avoid, persist through difficulties, and ultimately achieve better outcomes.

For example, a Stanford study on teacher expectations explored teacher expectations and their effect on student performance. Teachers were told that certain students were "academic bloomers," leading them to unconsciously treat these students differently, with higher expectations and more encouragement. As a result, these students showed significantly greater academic improvement compared to their peers. This study highlights how a teacher's beliefs and encouraging words can influence student achievement (Rosenthal & Jacobson, 1968).

When teachers believe in their students' potential, it creates a positive feedback loop. Students who sense this belief are more likely to develop a growth mindset—the understanding that their abilities can improve through effort and learning. This mindset fuels resilience, making students more likely to push through academic challenges, whether they're mastering a difficult concept or improving a skill that doesn't come naturally.

The impact extends beyond academic performance. Students who feel supported and believed in also tend to have higher self-esteem, better relationships with peers and teachers, and a more positive attitude toward learning. These students are more engaged in the classroom, participate more actively in discussions, and are more likely to take intellectual risks, all critical factors in deep learning and long-term academic success.

For teachers and schools, this creates a win-win situation. Students who perform better contribute to a more vibrant, dynamic learning environment. Higher student achievement also reflects positively on the school, demonstrating the effectiveness of its teaching methods and creating a culture of success. Furthermore, when students succeed, it reinforces teachers' confidence in their ability to make a difference, leading to greater job satisfaction and a more motivated teaching staff.

Ultimately, the belief in students' potential not only enhances their academic performance but also contributes to a positive, thriving educational environment where both students and teachers can excel. This holistic success benefits the entire school community, making it a powerful tool for achieving educational goals.

In 2014, while serving as a school principal, I encountered a moment that highlighted the profound impact of a teacher's beliefs on their students. During a faculty meeting, one teacher openly stated that, given the challenges faced by our student population at the 99% Title I school— high poverty, low socio-economic status, and predominantly single-parent homes—the highest achievement she could envision for the students was perhaps becoming a manager at the local gas station. This statement not only revealed her deeply rooted beliefs about our students but also reflected the level of teaching and expectation she communicated to them. There is nothing demeaning about becoming a manager at a local gas station. It takes great customer service, problem-solving, reading, and mathematical skills to handle a management position. However, our words should not limit possibilities. If we, as educators, allow our words to be limited by stereotypes and low expectations, we risk capping the potential of those who are meant to go beyond average.

Every student enters the classroom with a unique set of strengths, challenges, and experiences. Some may struggle with math, while others may excel in art. Some may face personal hardships that impact their academic performance, while others may thrive in a stable environment. Regardless of these differences, the belief that every student can grow enables us to meet them where they are and guide them toward where they can be.

Seeing Beyond Labels

One of the greatest obstacles to recognizing the potential for growth in every student is the tendency to label them based on their current performance or behavior. Labels such as "struggling," "gifted," "lazy," or "troublemaker" can create fixed expectations that limit both the student and the teacher. These labels can become self-fulfilling prophecies, shaping the way we interact with students and the opportunities we provide them.

Avoid letting the opinions of a previous year's teacher shape your expectations of your students in the new school year. Remember, a student's (mis)behavior with one teacher does not dictate how they will behave with you, especially if you have created a voice-activated classroom. Your life-giving words are powerful enough to transform the behavior of any student, even those who have been unfairly labeled "bad."

To truly see the potential for growth in every student, we must look beyond these labels. We must understand that a student's current state is not their final state. A struggling reader can become an avid one with the right support and encouragement. A disruptive student can channel their energy into leadership roles. By focusing on growth rather than fixed traits and by applying the voice-activated formula with consistency and fidelity, we open the door to endless possibilities.

Creating a Supportive Environment

Believing in the potential for growth also means creating an environment that supports and nurtures this growth. This involves setting high expectations while providing the necessary support to meet them. It means offering encouragement and constructive feedback, fostering a sense of belonging and safety, and recognizing and celebrating progress, no matter how small.

In my own classroom, I have witnessed the transformative power of a supportive environment. I remember a student—Crystal—who struggled with math. She often felt defeated and disengaged. Instead of labeling her "bad at math," I chose to believe in her potential to improve. I would whisper phrases such as "I believe in you" and "Good morning, my little mathematician" in her ear. This made Crystal's face light up, and I could see her confidence exude in her posture. I provided extra support, celebrated her small victories, and encouraged her to adopt a growth mindset. Over time, Crystal's confidence grew, and so did her skills. By the end of the year, she had made significant progress, not just in math but in her overall attitude toward learning.

The Ripple Effect of Belief

The belief in every student's potential to grow does not only affect individual students; it has a ripple effect that can transform entire classrooms and schools. When teachers collectively embrace the belief that "every student has the potential to grow, learn, and succeed," it fosters a culture of high expectations, mutual respect, and continuous improvement. Students begin to believe in their own potential and in each other's. This creates a positive feedback loop, where success breeds confidence, and confidence breeds further success; a.k.a. 'The Ripple Effect of Belief." Let's cause a ripple effect across the world!

Cultivating Positive Expectations

When we approach our students with the belief that they are capable, intelligent, and eager to learn, we set the stage for these qualities to emerge. Positive expectations act as a magnet, drawing out the best in our students and encouraging them to rise to the occasion.

The energy we bring into the classroom is equally crucial. As teachers, we set an emotional tone for our students. Our enthusiasm, passion, and positive demeanor can create an environment that is conducive to learning and personal growth. When we approach our work with joy and a sense of purpose, it is contagious; students respond with increased engagement, motivation, and enthusiasm.

Consider the impact of starting each day with a positive ritual; perhaps a morning meeting where students share something good that has happened or something they are looking forward to. This practice not only fosters a sense of community but also sets a positive tone for the day. Similarly, maintaining a classroom atmosphere that celebrates successes, both big and small, reinforces a positive energy that attracts further achievements.

Visualization and Goal Setting

Encouraging students to visualize their success and set clear, attainable goals can help them attract the outcomes they desire. Visualization involves creating a mental image of achieving a specific goal, which can enhance motivation and focus.

For example, before a big test, guide your students through a visualization exercise where they imagine themselves confidently applying their learning to a task and receiving a high score. This practice can reduce anxiety and boost confidence. Additionally, helping students set SMART goals (Specific, Measurable, Achievable, Relevant, Time-bound) provides them with a clear roadmap to success and keeps their focus on positive outcomes.

When students feel valued, respected, and supported, they are more likely to exhibit positive behaviors and attitudes. This sense of community can be fostered through collaborative activities, peer support systems, and a culture of mutual respect.

Encouraging students to support each other's growth and celebrate each other's successes reinforces the positive energy within the classroom. For instance, implementing peer tutoring programs or group projects in which students can share their strengths and learn from one another can enhance collective positive energy. By creating a classroom environment where everyone feels included and valued, we attract a spirit of cooperation and mutual respect.

When a student is facing a difficult situation, such as struggling with a particular subject or experiencing a personal issue, our role is to provide support and encouragement. Remind them of their past successes and the progress they have made. Help them reframe challenges as learning experiences, and emphasize their ability to overcome difficulties with perseverance and a positive attitude.

I recall a student—let's call him Alex—who struggled with self-confidence and often felt overlooked. By consistently reinforcing his strengths, celebrating his progress, and encouraging him to set and achieve goals, Alex began to believe in his potential. His transformation inspired his classmates, who began to support and celebrate each other's successes more openly. The positive energy spread, creating a classroom environment in which every student felt empowered and motivated to strive for their best.

The belief that every student has the potential to grow is more than a guiding principle; it is a powerful force that shapes our actions, interactions, and ultimately, the futures of our students. As experienced and compassionate educators, it is our duty to hold fast to this belief, see beyond the labels, create supportive environments, and nurture the growth mindset within ourselves and our students. By doing so, we unlock the boundless potential that resides within every child, paving the way for them to achieve their dreams and become the best versions of themselves.

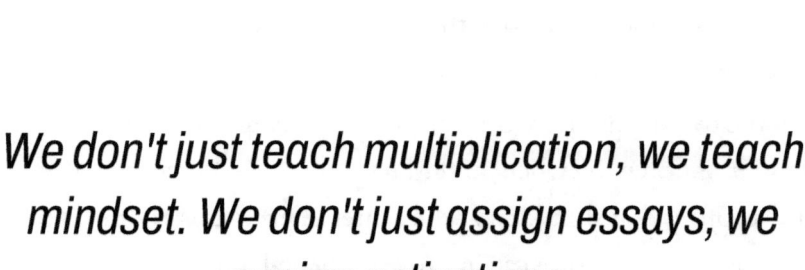

We don't just teach multiplication, we teach mindset. We don't just assign essays, we assign activations.

MINDSET SHIFTS

-wwwfwwww-

There is a science behind the soul-stirring truth we've known all along: words don't just carry sound. They carry power. And that power doesn't merely impact the atmosphere of a room—it alters the architecture of the brain.

In the transformative work Words Can Change Your Brain, neuroscientists Dr. Andrew Newberg and Mark Robert Waldman reveal a revelation so profound, it should sit at the center of every classroom: "The ways we choose to use our words can improve the neural functioning of the brain." Now pause and let that land. Every word spoken by teachers and students in classrooms either builds or breaks, wires or weakens, regulates or deregulates your students' brain activity. This is backed by neuroscience.

Thanks to neuroplasticity, the brain is malleable—it rewires itself based on repeated thoughts, experiences, and yes... words. Words are not passive. They are active agents of change that trigger neurochemical reactions, sending messages across synapses that either fortify new beliefs or reinforce old, limiting ones.

The Voice-Activated Classroom teaches students to talk to themselves in ways that rewire their brain for belief. We don't just teach multiplication—we teach mindset. We don't just assign essays—we assign activations. We create cultures where phrases like "I can do hard things,"

"I'm getting better every day," and "My voice matters" are not just class-room mantras. They are neurological construction sites where self-worth is rebuilt, one syllable at a time.

Mindset Shifts in Students

A mindset shift refers to a fundamental change in how students perceive themselves, their abilities, and their potential for growth. It involves moving from fixed beliefs—where intelligence and skills are seen as innate and unchangeable—to growth-oriented beliefs that emphasize effort, learning, and confidence that abilities can be developed over time.

Neuroplasticity plays a critical role in this transformation. As students begin to challenge old narratives and replace them with affirming, constructive language, their brains begin forming new neural pathways aligned with this updated belief system. Research by Dr. Carol Dweck, pioneer of the growth mindset theory, reveals that students who believe their abilities can be developed are more likely to embrace challenges, persist through difficulties, and achieve at higher levels. Likewise, neuroscience research has shown that repeated thoughts and behaviors can physically alter brain structure, strengthening the connections that support confidence, motivation, and resilience (Davidson & Begley, 2012). This means that teaching students to intentionally speak words that reflect possibility and growth doesn't just inspire—it literally reshapes their brains to support those new beliefs. The act of dismantling self-sabotage becomes both a cognitive and a biological breakthrough, empowering students to rewrite their inner narratives and step into the fullness of their potential.

Results and Benefits of a Shifted Mindset

When students experience a mindset shift facilitated by their teachers and him/herself, several benefits emerge:

1. From Fixed to Growth Mindset

A fixed mindset suggests that intelligence and talent are static traits, leading students to avoid challenges, give up easily, and feel threatened by others' success. In contrast, a growth mindset embraces the belief that abilities can be developed through dedication and hard work. Teachers can encourage this shift by praising effort rather than innate ability. For example, instead of saying, "You're so smart," a teacher might say, "I love how you approached that problem and didn't give up." This shift teaches students to value the learning process and persist through difficulties.

2. From Fear to Confidence

Fear in the classroom often stems from a fear of judgment, failure, or not meeting expectations. Teachers can counteract this mindset by using forward-thinking and supportive language. Instead of saying, "Don't get it wrong," they might say, "I believe in you. Give it a try. There's no wrong answer in learning." Consistent encouragement fosters a safe environment in which students feel comfortable taking risks and making mistakes, which are essential for learning. Over time, this helps build self-confidence and a willingness to tackle challenging tasks.

3. From Negative Self-Perception to Positive Self-Image

Negative self-perception can lead students to believe that they are not smart, capable, or worthy. Teachers can help reshape these self-beliefs by recognizing and affirming each student's unique strengths. For example, a student who may not excel in math yet but is a talented artist should hear, "Your creativity is a gift, and it adds so much to our class." When students are repeatedly exposed to positive reflections of themselves, they start internalizing these activations, leading to a more positive self-image.

4. From Disengagement to Motivation

Disengaged students often feel disconnected from their learning. Teachers can ignite motivation by showing enthusiasm for the content and conveying belief in each student's potential. Statements like "I can see your hard work, and it's paying off!" or "I'm excited to see what you'll do next!" help students feel that their efforts are recognized and valued. This kind of language fosters intrinsic motivation, where students are driven by their own growth and accomplishments rather than external rewards.

5. From Helplessness to Empowerment

Learned helplessness occurs when students believe they have no control over their outcomes, often due to repeated failures or negative feedback. To empower students, teachers need to shift their language to focus on effort, strategy, and choice. Phrases like "What strategy could you try next?" or "You can improve with practice" help students see themselves as active agents in their success. This fosters a sense of control and motivates them to take ownership of their learning.

6. From Isolation to Community

A sense of isolation can lead students to feel alienated or disconnected from their peers. Teachers can build a community mindset by using inclusive language and fostering collaboration. Statements like "We're all in this together" or "Let's support each other" encourage students to see themselves as part of a supportive network. This sense of belonging enhances engagement, cooperation, and empathy, making the classroom a more inclusive and harmonious place.

7. From Apathy to Purpose

When students do not see the relevance of their studies, they may become apathetic. Teachers can combat this by connecting learning to real-world applications or personal goals. For instance, "When you're planning a party and need to figure out how much food to buy for your guests, solving math problems helps you learn how to think critically. When you break down the numbers—like when you're figuring out how many pizzas to order based on how many people are coming—you develop skills that are super useful in real-life situations!" or "Writing skills can help you share your story with the world." By aligning educational content with students' interests and aspirations, teachers help students find meaning in their work, driving motivation and enthusiasm.

8. From Anxiety to Calm

Many students experience anxiety, whether from test pressures, social dynamics, or fear of failure. Teachers can help by using calm, reassuring language that acknowledges emotions while providing comfort and encouragement. Phrases like "It's okay to feel nervous. We're here to learn together" or "Let's take a deep breath and try again" can help de-escalate anxiety and create a classroom atmosphere that feels safe and supportive. This encourages students to participate more fully without fear of judgment.

9. From Defeat to Resilience

Students who experience setbacks may feel defeated and believe they cannot overcome challenges. Teachers can build resilience by reframing setbacks as opportunities for growth. Phrases like "What did we learn from this mistake?" or "Every step back is a step toward your comeback" help normalize failure as part of the learning process. Encouraging reflection and persistence instills a belief in students that they have the inner strength to keep trying, even when things are tough.

10. From Disinterest to Curiosity

A lack of curiosity often stems from rigid teaching methods that do not encourage exploration or creativity. By using language that invites inquiry, teachers can foster a classroom culture in which curiosity is cele-brated. Instead of saying, "This is what you need to know," teachers could ask, "What do you think will happen if...?" or "How would you solve this problem differently?" These types of questions encourage students to think critically, ask questions, and develop genuine interest in learning.

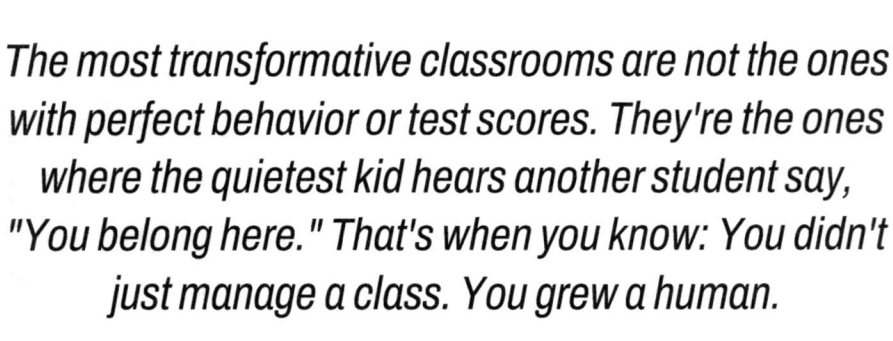

The most transformative classrooms are not the ones with perfect behavior or test scores. They're the ones where the quietest kid hears another student say, "You belong here." That's when you know: You didn't just manage a class. You grew a human.

CHAPTER 11

SPEAK TO GROW (SEL)

The classroom buzzed with the hum of small group work. Markers squeaked across poster boards. Laughter rippled from one table as a team debated how to present their idea. In the far corner, Maya sat frozen.

Her assignment lay untouched. Her breathing was shallow. She stared at the question, and the voice of anxiety began to whisper. She glanced around. Her peers were moving forward. Her thoughts were spiraling backward.

Then, as if on cue, her teacher noticed. Ms. Lane didn't correct. She connected. She walked over slowly, lowered herself to eye level, and said gently: "Breathe first. Then speak life to yourself, like we practiced."

Maya nodded—barely. She closed her eyes and whispered: "I can do hard things. My brain can grow. I am not my fear."

She exhaled. Picked up her pencil. And wrote one sentence.

Moments later, a classmate leaned over with a quiet smile and said: "Hey, that's a strong start." Maya looked up, surprised by the encouragement. Her classmate had remembered the peer voice-coding they practiced every Friday.

By the end of the period, Maya had written more than she thought possible. She had not only finished the task—she had regulated her emotions, accepted support, taken a risk, and rebuilt belief in herself.

That is SEL in action. And none of it required a scripted lesson. It required:

▶ A teacher who could recognize the signs of internal struggle (self-awareness)

▶ A moment to re-center with positive inner dialogue (self-management)

▶ A peer who chose compassion over competition (social awareness)

▶ A classroom culture that normalized support and safety (relationship skills)

▶ A student brave enough to try again when it felt easier to give up (responsible decision-making)

This is what happens when a classroom becomes Voice-Activated.

When phrases aren't fluff.

When breathing is strategy.

When students are taught that their voice carries power.

This is Social Emotional Learning—not just explained but spoken into motion. Social Emotional Learning (SEL) is the lifelong process by which children and adults learn to:

▶ Understand and manage their emotions

▶ Set and achieve meaningful goals

▶ Feel and show empathy for others

▶ Establish and maintain healthy relationships

▶ Make responsible and caring decisions

The leading organization behind SEL in education is CASEL (the Collaborative for Academic, Social, and Emotional Learning). CASEL has identified five core competencies that serve as the foundation of a student's emotional and social growth:

1. Self-Awareness
2. Self-Management
3. Social Awareness
4. Relationship Skills
5. Responsible Decision-Making

The Voice-Activated Classroom Meets SEL

In this classroom, words aren't just for instruction—they're the main ingredients for transformation. In a Voice-Activated Classroom, the atmosphere we create, the words we speak, and the language we model all combine to form a classroom culture that uplifts SEL.

In a Voice-Activated Classroom, we don't just teach SEL—we speak it into being.

We speak calm. We speak courage. We speak community. And we teach our students to do the same—for themselves and for each other. Because the most transformative classrooms are not the ones with perfect behavior or test scores. They're the ones where the quietest kid hears another student say, "You belong here." That's when you know: You didn't just manage a class. You grew a human.

SPEAK TO GROW: A Philosophy and a Practice

Speak to Grow is more than a method or classroom routine—it is a mindset, a philosophy, and a daily practice that believes words can cultivate growth in every dimension of a student's development. At its core, this belief confirms that the language we use—both as educators and as students—has the power to build the emotional, social, and relational foundation upon which learning stands.

In a Voice-Activated Classroom, we use our words not only to instruct, but to inspire growth in the five essential areas of Social Emotional Learning:

▸ **Emotional Intelligence**: Words help students recognize and name their emotions with clarity and confidence, fostering emotional literacy and regulation.

▸ **Personal Accountability**: Language becomes a tool for reflection, allowing students to own their actions and choices through guided self-talk and teacher modeling.

▸ **Peer Empathy and Respect**: Through intentional dialogue, students learn to uplift, include, and support one another in moments of success and struggle.

▸ **Internal Self-Regulation**: Phrases such as "I can stay calm" or "This is hard, but I can handle it" become self-activated scripts that students use to navigate stress and uncertainty.

▸ **A Culture of Collective Care**: When speaking life becomes a shared responsibility, the entire classroom begins to operate as a safe, supportive, emotionally intelligent community.

And here's the key distinction:

Teachers are not the only ones responsible for creating this culture.

In a truly voice-activated classroom, students also become voice-activators.

They don't simply receive encouragement—they learn how to *give it.*

They don't just internalize life-producing phrases—they become the source of these phrases for their peers.

It's one thing when a teacher says, *"You belong here."*

It's another when a student turns to a classmate and says, *"I believe in you."*

Those peer-to-peer interactions are not accidental—they are intentional outcomes of a classroom culture that prioritizes social emotional learning through language. When students are taught how to express empathy, resolve conflict with respect, and offer words that heal rather than harm, they don't just learn SEL—they live it.

When a child says:

▶ *"You can try again. I'll help you."*
▶ *"That wasn't kind—let's fix it together."*
▶ *"I noticed you were alone—want to join us?"*

They are not performing—they are practicing humanity.

They are not quoting a lesson—they are embodying it.

This is the true goal of Speak to Grow: to empower students not only to develop their own social emotional skills, but to use their voice as a tool of growth for those around them.

When students learn that their words hold power—when they realize they can build a classmate's courage with a sentence, or shift someone's day with a simple act of kindness— they step into leadership, empathy, and shared accountability.

And that is when a classroom becomes more than a space for learning.

It becomes a space for becoming.

Speak to Grow is not something we add to the curriculum. It is something we embed in our culture. It happens through hallway conversations, group work reflections, morning check-ins, and quick verbal coding between peers. It is modeled by the teacher, but multiplied by the students.

When students speak to grow, they help shape a classroom where belonging is felt, emotions are honored, voices are valued, and growth is inevitable.

Because when our words are intentional, our students become empowered.

And when students are empowered, everyone grows.

Reflection Questions for Teachers

Use the following questions to reflect on how your words—and your students' words—are shaping the social emotional climate of your classroom:

1. When was the last time you intentionally used your words to build a student's emotional confidence? What did you say? How did they respond?

2. Do your students regularly hear language that supports emotional regulation, accountability, and empathy? If not, what phrases can you begin modeling daily?

3. How often do you invite students to speak encouragement or voice-activations to each other?

4. What opportunities do students currently have to express their voice in ways that uplift their peers? Could those opportunities be expanded?

5. If an outsider walked into your classroom, would they *hear* a culture of care? What words would they overhear most often?

6. How can your classroom routines or norms more intentionally integrate "speaking to grow" as a shared responsibility?

Student Activity: Peer Voice Builders

Objective:

To develop peer-to-peer emotional intelligence and empathy through intentional language amongst classmates.

Activity Name: *"Speak Life Circle"*

When to Use:

Morning meetings, end-of-week wrap-ups, peer appreciation days, or moments of classroom conflict or tension.

Instructions:

1. **Form a Circle** – Gather students in a circle (or arrange in rows for large classes).

2. **Model the Language** – Begin with 2-3 sentence starters on the board or chart paper. Examples:

   - "One thing I admire about you is..."
   - "This week, I saw you..."
   - "You made a difference when you..."
   - "I believe in you because..."

3. **Pass the Voice** – One student begins by selecting a peer and offering a short phrase using one of the sentence starters. Then the peer responds with a "thank you" and continues by speaking to someone else.

4. **Anchor the Activity** – Close with a class phrase said aloud together, such as:

   "Our words build our classroom. Our voices lift each other. We speak to grow."

Teacher Tip:
Reinforce that students don't need to wait for the "circle" to use these phrases. Encourage them to use voice-builder statements throughout the day—during group work, transitions, etc.

Habits are sustainable when accountability is a part of the process.

CHAPTER 12
ACTIVATE EVERY DAY

-ᴡⱴⱳⱴⱴⱳᴡ-

For Voice Activation to work, it cannot merely be the classroom goal—it must become the classroom habit. Goals expire. Habits endure. And when those habits are grounded in positive, intentional speech, they do more than shape culture—they rewire brains. Through the science of neuroplasticity, we now understand that repeated language—especially life-producing language—strengthens the neural pathways associated with confidence, connection, and cognitive growth. In other words, the brain begins to believe what it hears most often. When affirming, empowering words are spoken regularly by both teachers and students, they shift from conscious effort to subconscious rhythm. This is how Voice- Activation becomes not just what we do, but who we are. It flows into every interaction, reshaping both classroom atmosphere and student identity at the level of the mind.

Developing this habit requires consistency and intentionality. It starts with self-awareness—being mindful of the words you speak to yourself and to your students—and it's followed by teaching students self-awareness, as they too should be mindful of the words they speak to themselves and to others. It also demands reflection: Are your words building confidence, sparking curiosity, and inspiring growth, or are they unintentionally limiting potential? The more teachers practice speaking life into their students—and the more students practice speaking life into themselves, their peers, and their environment—the more effortless it becomes. Why? Because repeated language patterns literally reshape the brain. Through the power of neuroplasticity, these life-giving words carve new neural pathways, making positivity not just a choice but a cognitive default. Over time, what was once intentional becomes instinctive, reinforcing a classroom culture where uplifting language isn't the exception—it's the expectation.

Habitual Voice Activation has a ripple effect. When students hear forward-thinking words daily, they internalize them and begin to replicate the behavior. Over time, this creates a community of learners who uplift and empower one another. Teachers who master this habit witness the transformation not only in their students but also in their own sense of purpose and fulfillment. After all, true change doesn't come from a one-time effort; it comes from a lifetime of intentional, positive habits.

Drawing inspiration from James Clear's *Atomic Habits*, this chapter focuses on actionable strategies to make Voice Activation an effortless part of your teaching day.

Start Small and Build Momentum

One of the most important principles from *Atomic Habits* is the idea of starting small. Clear writes, "Habits are the compound interest of self-improvement." The same applies to recoding your classroom's cultural DNA. Begin with connecting the first base from the "A" Strand to the first base of the "B" Strand. By connecting one base together each week to form a pair, a teacher can steadily construct the strands that make up the classroom culture they desire. Within six weeks, these incremental steps will form a transformative structure, a classroom's double helix, one that resonates positivity and empowerment.

Example:

▶ **Week 1:** Connect the 1ˢᵗ Base Pair – Teacher: Him/Herself

▶ **Week 2:** Connect the 2ⁿᵈ Base Pair – Teacher: Atmosphere

▶ **Week 3:** Connect the 3ʳᵈ Base Pair – Teacher: Students

▶ **Week 4:** Connect the 4ᵗʰ Base Pair – Student: Him/Herself

▶ **Week 5:** Connect the 5ᵗʰ Base Pair – Student: Peers

▶ **Week 6:** Connect the 6ᵗʰ Base Pair – Whole Class: Atmosphere

"A" Strand		*"B" Strand*	
	Teacher		Him/Herself
	Teacher		Atmosphere
	Teacher		Student(s)
	Student(s)		Him/Herself
	Student(s)		Peers
	Whole Class		Atmosphere

Starting small will help you avoid feeling overwhelmed while building the foundation for a sustainable habit.

Make It Obvious

James Clear emphasizes the principle of making habits "obvious" to ensure they are difficult to ignore and easy to adopt. The idea is simple: the clearer and more visible a habit is in your environment, the more likely you are to follow through. This concept highlights the power of environmental design and intentionality in habit formation.

For example, if your goal is to drink more water, keeping a water bottle in plain sight on your desk acts as a constant visual reminder. Similarly, in a classroom setting, a teacher could place daily Life-Producing Words / Phrases cards on each student's desk to reinforce the habit of starting the day with empowering words. The key is to reduce friction between you and the desired action by aligning your environment with obvious reminders.

Additionally, making positive words a visible part of the classroom's physical and social structure helps set the tone. A "Words Have Power" bulletin board could feature student-generated phrases or testimonials about how words have impacted their lives. These tangible reminders make the habit of using positive language unavoidable and central to the classroom culture.

By designing environments and routines to make positive, voice-activated habits obvious, teachers can rewire the classroom dynamics. This approach ensures that powerful, voice-activating language becomes not just a practice but an integral part of the classroom DNA, creating a space where students thrive academically, emotionally, and socially.

Anchor It to an Existing Routine

Another powerful technique from James Clear's *Atomic Habits* is **"habit stacking,"** the practice of pairing a new habit with an existing one to make it easier to adopt. By anchoring Voice Activation to established routines, it seamlessly integrates the concept into your teaching day without adding extra complexity, recoding your classroom's DNA at the same time.

Identify Natural Pairing Points

Look for moments in your teaching routine where Voice Activation can fit naturally. For example:

▶ **During Morning Greetings:** As students walk into the classroom, greet each one with a positive personalized phrase that uplifts their mood and sets the tone for the day.

▶ **Starting Class:** Begin each lesson with life-producing phrases, either by delivering teacher-led statements or by asking students to recite their own phrases.

Link It to Your Current Practices

Find ways to align Voice Activation with things you already do:

▶ If you start the day by taking attendance, use that moment to say an encouraging phrase to the class.

▶ If you are on duty on the hallway twice a week, use that moment to speak life to students who pass you.

Leverage Classroom Signals

Utilize auditory or visual signals already in place, such as bells or timer, as cues for Voice Activation. For instance:

▶ When the bell rings to start a period, pair it with a brief activation.

▶ When setting a timer for an activity, remind students, "You have what it takes to meet this challenge."

By anchoring Voice Activation to these existing routines, you create consistent opportunities to infuse positive, uplifting language into your classroom culture. Over time, both you and your students will naturally align your speech and actions with the activating energy these practices bring.

Focus on Identity, Not Outcomes

Clear writes, "The ultimate form of intrinsic motivation is when a habit becomes part of your identity." To make Voice Activation stick, see yourself as a teacher who speaks life. Internalize the belief that your words have the power to shape the mindset, confidence, and future of every student in your classroom. When you identify as a teacher who uses positive language daily, your actions will align naturally with that identity.

Instead of focusing solely on immediate results, such as improved student behavior, concentrate on the long-term transformation you're creating. Remember, you're not just managing a classroom—you're building a culture of encouragement and empowerment.

Overcome Obstacles with a Plan

Inevitably, challenges will arise. You may have days when stress, frustration, or fatigue make it harder to stay positive. Anticipating these obstacles and creating a plan can help you stay on track. For instance:

▶ When feeling overwhelmed, take a moment to breathe deeply and silently encourage yourself, thinking phrases such as "I am equipped, and I am graced with the wisdom and peace to handle this obstacle."

▶ If a student's behavior disrupts the flow, remind yourself of the power of reframing. Instead of saying, "Why can't you focus?" try, "How can I help you focus better?"

▶ On particularly hard days, lean on your support system—colleagues who share your commitment to positivity.

Having strategies in place will ensure that setbacks don't derail your progress.

Track and Celebrate Your Progress

Habits thrive when they're measurable. Create a simple system to track your Voice Activation practice. This could be as straightforward as a checklist on your planner or a quick note in your teaching journal about a moment when your words made an impact. Reflecting on these wins, no matter how small, will reinforce your commitment to the habit.

Celebrate your progress, too. Acknowledge how far you've come, and take pride in the positive energy you're creating for your students. Your celebration doesn't have to be elaborate; even pausing to smile and say, "Today, I connected the 5th and the 6th Base Pair together" can be enough.

Make It a Team Effort: Accountability at Every Level

Habits are more sustainable when accountability is part of the process. Start by finding a fellow teacher to partner with. Invite them to observe your classroom for 10 minutes to provide constructive feedback on how effectively you're using Voice Activation techniques and fostering a positive atmosphere. Their outside perspective can offer valuable insights and help you stay on track.

Once you've connected all the bases of the "A" Strand and the "B" Strand together, extend accountability to your students. Teach them to hold each other accountable by speaking life-giving words to each other, sharing activations, or offering encouragement at the start or end of the class. You can also empower your students to hold you accountable, encouraging them to share when they notice the positive effects of your words or when they feel more encouraged and supported.

By making accountability a shared responsibility among teachers and students, you'll foster a strong, collaborative community where everyone is invested in creating a culture of positivity and empowerment.

Sticking with Voice Activation every day is not about perfection; it's about persistence. As James Clear reminds us, "Success is the product of daily habits—not once-in-a-lifetime transformations." By starting small, making it obvious, and focusing on identity, you'll create a sustainable practice that transforms your classroom into a space where words uplift, encourage, and inspire. Remember, your words have the power to change lives—one habit at a time.

Conclusion of Part II

▸ **Beneath every unmotivated student lies an unmet need and an unheard voice.** Intentional words can awaken the dormant drive within students—not by force, but by faith, connection, and consistent voice-activating phrases.

▸ **You can't give what you don't have.** A teacher's emotional reservoir is directly linked to the classroom atmosphere. When educators pour from a full cup, they overflow with patience, creativity, and life-giving words that nourish every learner.

▸ **Words shape belief, and belief shapes outcomes.** Language fuels belief, and belief births achievement. Plant possibility through declarations, ultimately watching students rise into their spoken identity.

▸ **Mindset is not fixed—it's flexible**, and words are the tool that code it. Teachers are neural architects, who use language to rewire thought patterns and shift students from defeatist thinking to empowered learning.

▸ **Social and emotional learning thrives on intentional speech.** Embed SEL through life-producing phrases, peer-to-peer dialogue, and by implementing Speak to Grow—proving that emotional intelligence is not taught in silence, but in voice.

▸ **Daily words create daily worlds.** Activate growth, unity, and excellence with consistency. From morning greetings to classroom chants, every day becomes a new opportunity to speak transformation into existence.

APPENDIX

APPENDIX A

Prayers for Teachers

- Back to School Prayer
- Prayer for Wisdom
- Prayer for Guidance
- Prayer for Creativity
- Prayer for Patience
- "I feel like Quitting" Prayer
- Prayer for Unity Amongst Your Team / Faculty
- A Prayer Before Parent / Teacher Conferences
- A Holiday Prayer
- A Prayer for Your Health / Healing
- A Prayer for Behaviorally Challenged Students
- A Prayer for Peace in Your Home with your own children / grandchildren
- Prayer for the Campus Leader
- Prayer for Strength
- "I'm Getting Observed Today" Prayer
- Prayer of Gratitude
- 9-1-1 Prayer
- Prayer for a Fresh Anointing
- Financial Breakthrough Prayer
- "I'm Overwhelmed" Prayer

BACK TO SCHOOL PRAYER

Heavenly Father,

As we embark on this new school year, we come before You with grateful hearts and open spirits. We thank You for the calling You've placed upon each of us to be educators, to shape minds, and to inspire hearts. Lord, we ask for Your divine wisdom and guidance to be upon us every single day.

Father, we know that You have equipped us with everything we need to make a difference in our students' lives. We pray for Your strength when the days get long and challenging. Let Your peace fill our hearts and minds, so we can remain calm and focused, knowing that we are never alone.

Lord, give us eyes to see the potential in every student. Help us to speak words of encouragement and life into them, words that will uplift and motivate them to reach their full potential. May we be instruments of Your love, showing kindness and patience in every interaction.

We ask for Your protection over our schools. Surround our classrooms with Your angels, keeping all harm and negativity far from us. Let Your light shine brightly in our schools, creating an environment where respect, learning, and growth can flourish.

Father, we believe that this year will be our best year yet. We declare that we will see breakthroughs, that students will excel, and that lives will be transformed. We trust in Your promise that You have plans to prosper us, to give us hope and a future.

Thank You, Lord, for the opportunity to serve as teachers. We commit this school year into Your hands, knowing that with You, all things are possible.

In Jesus' name, we pray, Amen.

A PRAYER FOR WISDOM

Heavenly Father,

We come before You today, seeking Your divine wisdom and guidance. As teachers, we acknowledge that we cannot do this alone. We need Your insight, your clarity, and Your direction in every step we take.

Lord, Your Word says that if we lack wisdom, we should ask You, and You will give it generously without finding fault. So today, we ask for an abundant outpouring of Your wisdom. Fill our minds with knowledge and our hearts with understanding. Help us to discern the best ways to reach and teach our students, to unlock their potential, and to inspire them to greatness.

Father, give us the wisdom to navigate the challenges we face, both in the classroom and in our interactions with colleagues and parents. Let us see every problem as an opportunity for growth and every obstacle as a chance to rely on Your strength.

Grant us the wisdom to be patient and compassionate, to listen more and speak less, to understand more and judge less. May our words be seasoned with grace, lifting up and encouraging those around us.

Lord, we know that every child in our classroom is a precious gift from You. Give us the wisdom to see their unique strengths and to help them overcome their weaknesses. Show us how to create an environment where every student feels valued, respected, and motivated to learn.

We thank You, Father, for the privilege of shaping young minds and hearts. We trust that with Your wisdom, we can make a lasting impact. Guide our decisions, our plans, and our actions, so that everything we do brings glory to Your name.

In Jesus' name, we pray, Amen.

A PRAYER FOR GUIDANCE

Heavenly Father,

We come before You today, seeking Your divine guidance in our roles as teachers. We acknowledge that without Your direction, our efforts can fall short. We need Your presence to lead us, to inspire us, and to guide us every step of the way.

Lord, we ask for Your light to illuminate our path. Show us the way to connect with each of our students, to understand their needs, and to nurture their growth. Give us the insight to see beyond the surface, recognize their unique gifts, and help them overcome their challenges.

Father, grant us the discernment to make wise decisions in our classrooms. Guide us in creating a learning environment that is both stimulating and supportive. Help us to balance structure with creativity, discipline with encouragement, and teaching with listening.

We pray for Your wisdom in our interactions with colleagues, parents, and the wider school community. Let us be instruments of Your peace, fostering collaboration and unity. Give us the words to speak in difficult situations and the grace to handle every challenge with patience and love.

Lord, we ask for Your strength to sustain us through the demands of our profession. When we feel overwhelmed, remind us of Your promise that You are our refuge and strength, an ever-present help in trouble. Renew our spirits daily, so that we can approach each new day with enthusiasm and dedication.

Heavenly Father, guide us to be the best versions of ourselves, reflecting Your love and wisdom in all that we do. May our actions and words inspire our students to strive for excellence, to believe in themselves, and to reach for their dreams.

Thank You, Lord, for the incredible privilege and responsibility of teaching. We trust in Your guidance and place this school year in Your hands, knowing that with You, all things are possible.

In Jesus' name, we pray,

Amen.

A PRAYER FOR CREATIVITY

Heavenly Father,

We come before You with grateful hearts, seeking Your divine inspiration and creativity. As teachers, we desire to ignite a passion for learning in our students, to open their minds to new possibilities, and to make each lesson an adventure.

Lord, You are the ultimate Creator, the One who designed the heavens and the earth with such intricate beauty and detail. We ask that You pour out Your creative spirit upon us. Fill our minds with fresh ideas and innovative approaches that will capture our students' imaginations and engage their hearts.

Father, give us the creativity to make our classrooms vibrant and dynamic places of learning. Help us to see beyond traditional methods and embrace new ways of teaching that cater to the diverse needs and learning styles of our students. Let our lessons be not only informative but also inspiring, sparking a lifelong love for knowledge and discovery.

Grant us the wisdom to use creativity to solve problems and overcome challenges. When resources are limited or time is short, show us how to think outside the box and find effective solutions. Let our creativity be a source of joy and motivation for our students, helping them to see that learning can be fun and exciting.

Lord, we pray for the courage to take risks and try new things, knowing that You are with us every step of the way. Help us to create an environment where students feel safe to express themselves, to ask questions, and to explore their own creativity.

Father, let our creativity reflect Your love and grace, touching the lives of our students in meaningful ways. May we inspire them to dream big, to believe in their abilities, and to pursue their passions with confidence.

Thank You, Lord, for the incredible privilege of teaching. We trust in Your boundless creativity to guide us and to make this school year extraordinary.

In Jesus' name, we pray,

Amen.

A PRAYER FOR PATIENCE

Heavenly Father,

We come before You with humble hearts, seeking Your divine patience in our roles as teachers. We acknowledge that teaching is a profound calling, filled with both joys and challenges. We need Your grace to navigate each day with the calm and steadfastness that only You can provide.

Lord, we ask for an abundance of patience, the kind that mirrors Your endless patience with us. Help us to remain calm in the face of disruptions, to respond with kindness when frustration arises, and to offer understanding when our students struggle.

Father, give us the patience to listen more than we speak, to understand more than we judge, and to encourage more than we criticize. Let our interactions be filled with compassion, allowing our students to feel valued and heard.

Grant us the strength to endure the daily demands of teaching with grace and perseverance. When we feel overwhelmed, remind us of Your promise that You are our refuge and strength, an ever-present help in times of need. Renew our spirits daily, so that we can approach each new day with a heart full of patience and a mind focused on our purpose.

Lord, we ask for Your guidance in managing our time and our energy, so that we can give our best to our students without losing sight of our own well-being. Help us to find moments of peace and reflection, where we can recharge and renew our commitment to our calling.

Heavenly Father, let our patience be a testament to Your love, reflecting Your kindness and mercy in all that we do. May our students see in us a living example of Your grace, inspiring them to treat others with the same patience and understanding.

Thank You, Lord, for the incredible privilege of shaping young minds and hearts. We trust in Your endless patience to guide us and to make this school year a time of growth and learning for both our students and ourselves.

In Jesus' name, we pray,

Amen.

"I FEEL LIKE QUITTING" PRAYER

Heavenly Father,

Right now, I come before You feeling worn out and overwhelmed. The weight of this journey has me questioning if I can keep going. I feel like quitting, Lord, but I know deep down that You have a purpose for me here.

Father, remind me why I started this journey. Help me to see the bigger picture and to understand that the impact I'm making goes beyond what I can see right now. Give me the strength to push through these challenging moments, to rise above the frustration, and to keep moving forward.

Lord, I need Your presence to surround me. Fill me with Your peace that surpasses all understanding. Help me to find rest in You, to lean on Your everlasting arms, and to draw strength from Your unfailing love. When I feel like I can't take another step, remind me that You are with me, carrying me through.

Father, renew my spirit and restore my passion. Ignite the fire within me that first led me to this calling. Help me to see my students through Your eyes, to remember that each one is a precious soul deserving of love, patience, and encouragement.

Guide me to find balance, Lord. Show me how to take care of myself while caring for others. Help me to set healthy boundaries and to seek moments of rest and rejuvenation. Let me not be afraid to ask for help, to lean on my community, and to trust that You are my ultimate source of strength.

Lord, when the days are long, and the challenges seem insurmountable, remind me of Your promises. You said that You would never leave me nor forsake me, and I stand on that truth today. Give me the courage to keep going, the wisdom to know when to rest, and the grace to face each day with hope and determination.

Thank You, Father, for Your unwavering support and love. I trust that with You by my side, I can overcome any obstacle. I declare that I will not quit, for You are my refuge and my strength.

In Jesus' name, I pray,

Amen.

PRAYER FOR UNITY AMONGST YOUR TEAM / FACULTY

Heavenly Father,

We come before You as one body, united in our purpose and calling. We lift up our team, our faculty, and our school community, asking for Your divine unity to bind us together. Lord, we know that we are stronger together, and we seek Your presence to guide us into deeper harmony and collaboration.

Father, we ask that You remove any barriers that stand in the way of our unity. Heal any wounds from past misunderstandings or conflicts. Replace any spirit of division with Your spirit of peace and love. Help us see each other through Your eyes, with grace and compassion, and recognize the unique gifts and strengths that each person brings to our team.

Lord, we pray for open and honest communication among us. Let us speak with kindness and listen with empathy. When challenges arise, give us the wisdom to navigate them with a spirit of cooperation and mutual respect. May we support and uplift one another, always seeking the best for our colleagues and our students.

Father, we ask for a spirit of collaboration to flourish within our team. Help us to work together seamlessly, each playing our part in creating an environment where our students can thrive. Let our unity be a beacon of Your love, shining brightly for all to see. May our united efforts bring about positive change and lasting impact in our school and beyond.

Lord, we pray for Your blessing over our team meetings, our planning sessions, and our daily interactions. Let Your presence be felt in every decision we make and every action we take. Fill us with Your creativity, Your wisdom, and Your strength, so that we can accomplish more together than we ever could alone.

Heavenly Father, we thank You for the privilege of serving alongside such dedicated and passionate individuals. We trust that as we unite in purpose and heart, You will lead us to new heights and greater achievements. We declare that our team will be a powerful force for good, reflecting Your love and unity in all that we do.

In Jesus' name, we pray,
Amen.

A PARENT / TEACHER CONFERENCE PRAYER

Heavenly Father,

We come before You with grateful hearts, ready to partner with parents for the well-being and growth of our students. As we prepare for these parent-teacher conferences, we ask for Your divine presence to fill the room, guiding every conversation and interaction.

Lord, we ask for Your wisdom to be upon us as teachers. Help us to see each student through Your eyes, recognizing their unique strengths and areas for growth. Give us the words to communicate clearly and effectively, offering insights that will help parents understand their child's progress and potential.

Father, grant us the patience and grace to listen attentively to the concerns and hopes of each parent. Let us approach these meetings with empathy and an open heart, ready to work together for the best interests of the child. Help us to build strong, trusting relationships with parents, fostering a sense of teamwork and collaboration.

Lord, we pray for Your peace to reign over these conferences. Let there be mutual respect and understanding, even in challenging conversations. May our words be seasoned with kindness and encouragement, uplifting and inspiring both parents and students.

Heavenly Father, we ask for Your guidance in setting goals and creating action plans that will support each student's academic and personal growth. Help us to identify practical steps and resources that will empower parents to be active partners in their child's education.

Thank You, Lord, for the opportunity to work alongside parents in shaping the minds and hearts of their children. We trust in Your promise that with You, all things are possible. We declare that these conferences will be productive, positive, and filled with Your wisdom and love.

In Jesus' name, we pray,

Amen.

A HOLIDAY PRAYER

Heavenly Father,

As we approach this special holiday season, we come before You with hearts full of gratitude and joy. We thank You for the gift of teaching, for the privilege of shaping young minds, and for the opportunity to make a difference in the lives of our students.

Lord, we ask for Your blessings upon us during this holiday break. May it be a time of rest and rejuvenation. Refresh our spirits, renew our energy, and fill us with Your peace. Help us to find moments of joy and celebration with our loved ones, cherishing the time we have together.

Father, we pray for Your protection over our school community. Keep our students, their families, and our colleagues safe and healthy during this time. Surround us with Your love and grace, and let Your presence be felt in every home.

As we reflect on the year gone by, Lord, we are thankful for Your guidance and provision. We ask for Your continued wisdom as we look forward to the new year. Help us to carry the lessons we've learned and the growth we've experienced into the days ahead.

Lord, we lift up those who may be facing challenges or hardships during this season. Comfort those who are grieving, provide for those in need, and bring hope to those who feel discouraged. Use us as instruments of Your love and kindness, showing compassion and generosity to those around us.

Heavenly Father, we thank You for the blessings of this holiday season. May our hearts be filled with Your joy, our minds with Your peace, and our actions with Your love. Let us return to our classrooms renewed and inspired, ready to continue the important work You have called us to do.

In Jesus' name, we pray,

Amen.

A PRAYER FOR YOUR HEALTH / HEALING

Heavenly Father,

We come before You today with hearts full of faith, seeking Your healing touch over every aspect of our lives. As teachers, we carry the weight of many responsibilities, and we ask for Your divine intervention to bring health and healing to our bodies, minds, and spirits.

Lord, we pray for physical healing. You are the Great Physician, and we believe that Your power can restore our bodies to perfect health. Touch every ache, every pain, and every ailment with Your healing hands. Renew our strength and vitality so that we can continue to serve our students with energy and enthusiasm.

Father, we lift up our mental health to You. In the midst of our busy and often stressful lives, we ask for Your peace to calm our minds. Remove any anxiety, worry, or fear that may be weighing us down. Fill our minds with Your clarity, focus, and wisdom. Help us to find balance and prioritize our well-being so that we can think clearly and make sound decisions.

Lord, we also pray for emotional healing. You know the burdens we carry and the emotional toll that teaching can take. Comfort our hearts and heal any wounds from past hurts or disappointments. Fill us with Your joy and hope, reminding us of the purpose and passion that led us to this calling. Surround us with Your love and let it overflow into our interactions with others.

Heavenly Father, we ask for Your protection over our health, both now and in the days to come. Strengthen our immune systems and shield us from illness. Guide us to make healthy choices and to find moments of rest and rejuvenation.

Thank You, Lord, for the gift of healing that You offer so freely. We trust in Your promise that You are with us, that You care for us, and that You are working all things together for our good. We stand on Your word that says, "By His stripes, we are healed," and we declare Your healing power over our lives.

In Jesus' name, we pray,

Amen.

A PRAYER FOR BEHAVIORALLY CHALLENGED STUDENTS

Heavenly Father,

We come before You with hearts full of hope and compassion, lifting up our behaviorally challenged students into Your loving hands. Lord, You know each of their struggles, their fears, and their dreams. We ask for Your divine intervention in their lives, bringing healing, understanding, and transformation.

Father, we pray for Your guidance and wisdom as we work with these students. Help us to see beyond their behavior and to recognize the unique gifts and potential within each one. Give us the patience to understand their needs and the creativity to find effective ways to support and encourage them.

Lord, we ask for Your peace to fill their hearts and minds. Calm any storms of anger, frustration, or fear that may be causing their challenging behaviors. Replace those emotions with Your love and assurance, helping them to feel secure and valued.

We pray for Your strength to be upon us as educators. Equip us with the tools and strategies we need to address behavioral challenges with grace and effectiveness. Let our interactions be filled with kindness and empathy, creating an environment where these students can feel understood and supported.

Heavenly Father, we also lift up their families. Surround them with Your comfort and guidance and give them the strength to be a positive force in their child's life. Help us partner with them to create a consistent and loving support system for their children.

We declare Your favor and blessing over these students' lives. We believe in the power of Your transformative love to bring about positive change. Let them experience breakthroughs in their behavior, and may they grow into confident, resilient individuals who know their worth and potential.

Thank You, Lord, for Your grace and mercy. We trust in Your ability to work miracles in the lives of our students. We commit them to Your care, knowing that with You, all things are possible.

In Jesus' name, we pray,

Amen.

A PRAYER FOR PEACE IN YOUR HOME

Heavenly Father,

We come before You today with grateful hearts, seeking Your peace to fill our homes. As teachers, our days are filled with the challenges and joys of guiding our students, and we ask for Your tranquility to settle in our personal spaces, where we find rest and rejuvenation.

Lord, we invite Your presence into every room of our homes. Let Your peace, which surpasses all understanding, guard our hearts and minds. Remove any tension, stress, or conflict that may be present and replace it with Your calming grace.

Father, help us to create an environment of love and harmony. Teach us to communicate with kindness, to listen with empathy, and to support one another with patience and understanding. Let our homes be a sanctuary of peace, where we can find solace and renewal.

We pray for Your protection over our family relationships. Strengthen the bonds between us and guide us in resolving any disagreements with wisdom and grace. Let us approach each other with compassion and respect, nurturing a spirit of unity and support.

Lord, we also ask for Your peace to settle over our personal challenges and responsibilities. Help us to manage our tasks with a sense of calm and purpose, trusting in Your provision and guidance. May we find moments of stillness and reflection, allowing Your peace to wash over us and refresh our spirits.

Heavenly Father, we thank You for the gift of Your peace. We trust in Your promise to be with us always, to comfort us in times of need, and to bring harmony to our lives. We commit our homes into Your loving care, confident that with You, our lives will be filled with Your perfect peace.

In Jesus' name, we pray,

Amen.

PRAYER FOR THE CAMPUS & DISTRICT LEADERS

Heavenly Father,

We come before You today, lifting up our campus and district leaders into Your gracious hands. Lord, You have placed these individuals in positions of great responsibility, and we ask for Your divine guidance to be upon them as they lead and make decisions that impact our educational community.

Father, we pray for Your wisdom to flow through our leaders. Grant them the insight and clarity they need to navigate the challenges and opportunities they face. Help them to make decisions that are in the best interest of our students, teachers, and staff, always guided by Your truth and grace.

Lord, surround them with Your favor and strength. Let Your peace be their anchor amidst the pressures and demands of their roles. Encourage them when they feel weary and remind them of the purpose and calling You have placed upon their lives.

We ask for Your protection over their health and well-being. Keep them energized and focused and help them to find balance in their professional and personal lives. Let them be a source of inspiration and support to those around them, fostering a positive and productive environment for all.

Father, we also pray for unity and collaboration among our campus and district leaders. Let them work together with mutual respect and shared vision. Guide their conversations and interactions, so that they may build strong, effective teams that drive our schools toward excellence.

Heavenly Father, we thank You for the dedication and hard work of our leaders. We trust in Your ability to equip them with all they need to succeed and to lead with integrity and compassion. May their leadership reflect Your love and grace, making a lasting impact on our educational community.

In Jesus' name, we pray,

Amen.

A PRAYER FOR STRENGTH

Heavenly Father,

We come before You today, seeking Your divine strength to uplift and sustain us in our teaching journey. Lord, You know the demands and challenges we face each day, and we ask for Your powerful presence to fill us with renewed energy and courage.

Father, we pray for Your strength to be upon us in every moment. When we feel weary and overwhelmed, remind us of Your promise that Your grace is sufficient, and Your power is made perfect in our weakness. Fill us with Your boundless energy and unwavering resolve to continue our work with passion and purpose.

Lord, grant us the fortitude to overcome any obstacles that come our way. Equip us with the resilience to handle the pressures of our profession and the wisdom to address every challenge with grace and clarity. Let Your strength be our foundation, enabling us to face each day with confidence and determination.

We ask for Your peace to calm any anxieties or stress. Let Your presence be a comforting reminder that we are not alone in our efforts. Surround us with Your love and assurance and help us to find moments of rest and renewal amidst the busyness of our responsibilities.

Heavenly Father, we also pray for Your strength to inspire and uplift our students. Help us to be a source of encouragement and motivation, reflecting Your love and support in all that we do. Let our strength be a beacon of hope and resilience for those we serve.

Thank You, Lord, for the incredible privilege of teaching. We trust in Your power to sustain us, guide us, and empower us to make a positive impact. With You by our side, we know that we can achieve great things and continue to serve with heart and dedication.

In Jesus' name, we pray,

Amen.

"I'M GETTING OBSERVED TODAY" PRAYER

Heavenly Father,

Today, as I prepare to be observed in my classroom, I come before You with a heart full of faith and anticipation. Lord, I place this observation into Your hands, trusting that You will guide me through every moment with Your grace and wisdom.

Father, I ask for Your peace to envelop me. Calm any nerves or anxieties and fill me with confidence in the gifts and talents You have given me. Help me to focus on the students, the lesson, and the impact I am making rather than any external pressures or evaluations.

Lord, grant me clarity and creativity in delivering my lesson. Let Your presence shine through in my words and actions. May my teaching be a reflection of Your love and passion for learning, inspiring and engaging my students in meaningful ways.

I pray for Your favor during this observation. Let the observer see not just the content of the lesson but the dedication and commitment I bring to my role as an educator. Allow them to witness the positive environment I strive to create and the genuine connections I build with my students.

Father, I trust in Your promise that You are with me, guiding every step I take. Whether this observation goes as planned or presents unexpected challenges, remind me that Your grace is sufficient, and Your strength is perfect in my weakness.

Thank You, Lord, for the opportunity to showcase the work I am so passionate about. I commit this observation to You, knowing that with Your support, I can face it with confidence and poise.

In Jesus' name, I pray,

Amen.

PRAYER OF GRATITUDE

Heavenly Father,

Today, I come before You with a heart overflowing with gratitude. Lord, I thank You for the incredible privilege of being a teacher, for the opportunity to impact lives and to guide young minds on their journey of discovery.

Father, I am so grateful for Your constant presence and support in my role. Thank You for the wisdom and creativity You have blessed me with, enabling me to inspire and engage my students. Thank You for the strength You provide each day, helping me to meet the demands of this calling with grace and enthusiasm.

Lord, I am thankful for the joy and fulfillment that teaching brings into my life. I appreciate the moments of connection and growth with my students and the chance to witness their achievements and successes. Thank You for the support and encouragement from my colleagues and for the partnership we share in our mission to educate and uplift.

Father, I also give thanks for the challenges and opportunities for growth that come with this profession. They remind me to rely on Your strength and to seek Your guidance in all that I do. Thank You for teaching me patience, resilience, and the value of perseverance.

Heavenly Father, I am deeply thankful for the gift of every student who walks through my door. Each one is a unique blessing, and I am honored to be a part of their educational journey. Thank You for the chance to make a difference in their lives and for the privilege of watching them grow and thrive.

Lord, I trust in Your continued guidance and provision. As I move forward, I do so with a heart full of gratitude and a spirit ready to embrace each new day with joy and dedication.

In Jesus' name, I pray,

Amen.

9-1-1 PRAYER

Heavenly Father,

Right now, I come to You with a sense of urgency and faith, seeking Your divine protection and refuge. As Your Word in Psalm 91:1 promises, "He who dwells in the secret place of the Most High shall abide under the shadow of the Almighty." Lord, I claim that promise for myself and for all who serve in the field of education.

Father, I ask for Your shelter and safety over our classrooms, our schools, and our lives. In times of stress, challenge, or uncertainty, remind us that we are under Your mighty protection. Cover us with Your wings of grace and let Your presence be our stronghold and fortress.

Lord, when the pressures and demands of teaching feel overwhelming, help us to find solace in You. Let Your peace be our refuge and Your strength our anchor. Surround us with Your calming presence and let us feel Your comforting embrace in every moment of difficulty.

Father, we pray for Your protection over our physical health, our mental well-being, and our emotional stability. Keep us safe from harm, shield us from negativity, and guard us from any danger that might come our way. As we navigate the challenges of our profession, let us always feel secure in the knowledge that You are our protector.

Lord, we also lift up our students and their families. Surround them with Your care and guidance, and let Your protection cover them as well. Help us to create a safe and nurturing environment where they can thrive and grow.

Heavenly Father, thank You for being our ever-present help in times of need. We trust in Your promise of protection and embrace Your presence as our safe haven. With You by our side, we face each day with courage and confidence, knowing that we are shielded by Your mighty hand.

In Jesus' name, we pray,
Amen.

PRAYER FOR A FRESH ANOINTING

Heavenly Father,

Today, I come before You with a heart full of anticipation and faith, seeking a fresh anointing for every teacher. Lord, You are the source of all wisdom and grace, and we ask for Your divine touch to renew and empower us in our calling.

Father, we pray for a fresh outpouring of Your Spirit upon us. Ignite our passion anew and fill us with a renewed sense of purpose and energy. Let Your anointing flow through us, bringing creativity, inspiration, and joy to our teaching.

Lord, we ask for Your guidance in every lesson we prepare and every interaction we have. Let Your wisdom shine through us as we seek to educate and uplift our students. Equip us with fresh ideas, innovative approaches, and a deep sense of compassion, so that we may make a lasting impact in their lives.

Father, refresh our spirits and renew our strength. When we feel weary or challenged, let Your anointing be a source of revitalization and encouragement. Help us to overcome obstacles with grace and resilience, always leaning on Your strength and support.

Heavenly Father, we also pray for a fresh anointing of unity and collaboration among our colleagues. Let us work together in harmony and mutual support, inspired by Your Spirit, to create a positive and thriving educational environment.

Thank You, Lord, for the privilege of teaching and the opportunity to make a difference. We trust in Your promise that with Your anointing, we can achieve great things and fulfill our calling with excellence and dedication.

In Jesus' name, we pray,

Amen.

FINANCIAL BREAKTHROUGH PRAYER

Heavenly Father,

I come before You with a heart full of hope and faith, seeking Your divine intervention in my financial situation. Lord, You are my Provider, and I trust in Your promise to meet all my needs according to Your riches in glory.

Father, I ask for Your blessing and breakthrough in my finances. Open doors of opportunity and pour out Your abundance in my life. Help me to manage my resources wisely and to find new ways to increase my income. Guide me to make sound financial decisions and to steward Your blessings with gratitude and integrity.

Lord, I believe in Your power to bring about financial miracles. Whether it's through unexpected sources, creative ideas, or new opportunities, I trust that You are working on my behalf. Remove any barriers or limitations that have been holding me back and replace them with Your favor and provision.

Father, I also pray for Your peace to guard my heart and mind as I navigate financial challenges. Let me not be overwhelmed by worry or fear, but instead, let me be confident in Your promise to provide for all my needs. Strengthen my faith and remind me of Your faithfulness in every season.

Heavenly Father, I thank You for the blessings You have already bestowed upon me. I celebrate Your goodness and express my gratitude for the many ways You have provided in the past. I trust that with Your continued guidance and grace, I will experience a financial breakthrough that exceeds my expectations.

Thank You, Lord, for Your endless love and provision. I place my trust in You, knowing that You are more than capable of bringing about the breakthrough I need. With You by my side, I am confident in my journey towards financial stability and abundance.

In Jesus' name, I pray,

Amen.

I'M OVERWHELMED PRAYER

Heavenly Father,

I come before You today with a heart full of emotion, feeling overwhelmed by the many demands and responsibilities that weigh on me. Lord, You know the challenges I'm facing and the burdens I carry. I ask for Your divine intervention and peace to help me navigate through this season of overwhelm.

Father, I seek Your comfort and reassurance. Help me to release my worries and anxieties into Your loving hands. Let Your peace, which surpasses all understanding, flood my mind and heart. Remind me that I do not have to carry these burdens alone, for You are with me every step of the way.

Lord, grant me clarity and focus amidst the chaos. Guide me to prioritize and manage my tasks with grace and efficiency. Provide me with the strength and energy I need to meet each challenge with confidence and poise. When I feel weak or weary, renew my spirit and uplift my heart with Your unending grace.

Father, I pray for Your wisdom to navigate through the complexities of my responsibilities. Help me to find balance and seek support when needed. Surround me with encouragement and understanding, and let Your presence be a source of strength and comfort.

Heavenly Father, I thank You for Your constant love and faithfulness. Even in the midst of overwhelming moments, I trust in Your promise to be my refuge and strength. With You by my side, I know that I can overcome any obstacle and find peace amidst the storm.

Thank You, Lord, for Your boundless grace and for carrying me through these times. I place my trust in You, knowing that Your peace will guide me, and Your strength will sustain me.

In Jesus' name, I pray,

Amen.

A PRAYER FOR STANDARDIZED TESTING WEEK

Heavenly Father,

As we enter this week of standardized testing, I come before You with a heart full of faith, lifting up every student facing these exams. Lord, You know the effort and preparation that has gone into this moment, and I ask for Your blessings and guidance for each student.

Father, I pray for clarity of mind and calmness of spirit. Help the students to approach their tests with confidence and peace, free from anxiety and worry. Grant them the ability to recall and apply what they have learned, and let their focus be sharp and their thoughts clear.

Lord, we also ask for Your comfort and encouragement. Remind the students that their worth is not defined by their test scores but by Your love and grace. Help them to feel Your presence and trust in their abilities, knowing that they are supported and valued regardless of the outcome.

Father, I pray for strength and endurance throughout this testing week. Give the students the stamina they need to stay focused and alert and help them to manage their time and energy wisely. Surround them with a positive environment that fosters their best performance.

Heavenly Father, we also lift up the teachers and staff who are supporting the students through this process. Grant them wisdom, patience, and encouragement as they guide and assist the students. Let their efforts be fruitful and their impact be positive.

Thank You, Lord, for the opportunity to learn and grow. We trust in Your guidance and provision, and we commit this testing week into Your hands. May Your peace and strength be with each student, and may they find success and confidence in every challenge they face.

In Jesus' name, we pray,

Amen.

A Sneak Peek into The Voice-Activated Household

(Parent Edition)
Release Date: Early 2026

Chapter 1: "When Home Speaks, Hearts Listen"

A Sneak Peek into *The Voice-Activated Household* (Parent Edition)

By Dr. LaKesa B. Mitchell

Before your child ever steps into a classroom, they step into your voice. Not the loudest one. Not the sternest one. But the most consistent one.

The one that echoes through the walls at bedtime, spills across the breakfast table, and lingers long after you've walked away. The voice of the home. And whether we realize it or not, that voice shapes the beliefs, behaviors, and inner dialogue of our children—for better or for worse.

I still remember the day I realized my voice had more power than I thought. My son, five years old and full of wonder, stared at a puzzle scattered across the living room floor. He tried a few pieces. Got frustrated. Sat back and said, "I'm just not good at this. I'm not a puzzle person."

That wasn't his voice. That was mine.

It wasn't the exact phrase, but the undertone—the one I'd used too often when I was tired, impatient, or unaware of how much he was absorbing. "I'm not a morning person." "I'm just not organized like other moms." "I'll never figure this out."

That's when it hit me: our children don't just mimic our behaviors—they internalize our beliefs.

In The Voice-Activated Classroom, I taught educators how the words they speak can recode the DNA of their classrooms—rewiring students' beliefs, motivation, and even brain function. Now, I'm inviting parents to do the same. But this time, the classroom is your kitchen, your car rides, your hallway conversations. And the transformation begins with your voice.

Your Home Has a Language

Every household has its own language. It's not just the words—it's the emotional undertones, the nonverbal rhythms, the spoken and unspoken beliefs that govern the atmosphere.

Some homes speak peace. Others speak pressure. Some whisper "you matter" in a hundred tiny ways. Others unintentionally scream "you're not enough" through sarcasm, silence, or stress-fueled statements.

This book is about becoming fluent in the language of life-producing words.

The Science Behind the Sound

Words aren't just sounds. They're signals. And those signals send messages directly into the developing brains of children.

Neuroscience confirms that repeated language—especially from primary caregivers—shapes neural pathways. When your child hears, "You're so lazy" over and over, the brain doesn't filter that as a joke. It wires it as truth. When they hear, "I believe in you" even on hard days, it plants the seeds of resilience. Your words, quite literally, become your child's inner voice.

And just like a classroom can be rewired through intentional, powerful, emotionally intelligent language—so can your home.

The Voice-Activated Household Framework

Just like the classroom version, the Voice-Activated Household is built on six foundational bases that form the DNA of your home environment:

1. **Parent → Self**: What are the words you speak to yourself that spill over into your parenting?
2. **Parent → Child**: What do your children regularly hear from you, and how is it shaping their identity?
3. **Child → Self**: What internal dialogue is your child developing because of what's been spoken into them?
4. **Child → Sibling/Family**: How are your children learning to speak to one another?
5. **Parent(s) → Each Other**: What language is modeled between the adults in the home?
6. **Household → Atmosphere**: What kind of energy does your home radiate based on the language used inside of it?

Each of these strands plays a critical role in your home's culture. And together, they form a voice-activated ecosystem—a place where words either build or break, heal or harm, empower or discourage.

The Rewriting Starts Here

Here's what I know: You don't have to be a perfect parent to raise emotionally whole, confident, and resilient children. But you do have to be a conscious one. And that consciousness begins with your voice.

If you've spoken words in frustration, exhaustion, or fear—welcome to the club. We all have. But just like we can recode a classroom with new language, you can begin recoding your household today.

The moment you shift your language, you shift your legacy.

Let this chapter be your turning point—the moment you begin to speak not just to be heard, but to heal. To guide. To grow.

Because in the Voice-Activated Household, when home speaks, hearts listen—and generations change.

Sneak Peek into The Voice-Activated Life

Release Date: Summer of 2026

Chapter 1: "You Said It—Now You're Living It"

Sneak Peek from *The Voice-Activated Life*

By Dr. LaKesa B. Mitchell

There's a quiet force guiding your life. You use it every day—consciously or carelessly—with every conversation, every thought, every whispered complaint, and every bold declaration. It doesn't come in thunder or flashing lights. No, this force disguises itself in your everyday language. And yet, it holds the power to direct your destiny, build your relationships, shape your emotions, influence your health, and even rewrite your brain.

That force is your voice.

In my bestselling book *The Voice-Activated Classroom*, I taught educators how to transform their classrooms using one overlooked but powerful tool—their words. But I quickly realized this wasn't just a classroom principle. This was a *life* principle. From the boardroom to the living room, from morning routines to midnight prayers, our words aren't just noise—we are speaking *blueprints* into existence. Whether you're building peace or creating chaos, you're doing it with your words.

Let me be clear: You are not just describing your life with your words. **You are designing it.**

The Echo Chamber of Life

If your life feels stuck, chaotic, anxious, or uninspired, listen closely. Not to a podcast or a guru. Listen to *yourself*. Your life is always echoing what you've been saying.

Ever muttered, "I'm always behind," and noticed how you stay in a perpetual race with your to-do list? Ever said, "Nothing good ever happens to me," and found your days filling with small disappointments? Ever said, "I'm so tired of being overlooked," and then walk into rooms where no one acknowledges your presence?

That's not coincidence. That's *activation*.

Neuroscience calls this the **Reticular Activating System**—your brain's personal assistant. Whatever you consistently speak, your brain goes to work proving it to be true. You say it, and your mind filters the world to match it. Your body responds. Your decisions align. Your energy shifts. Your emotions follow.

You said it. Now you're living it.

The Double-Helix of Belief and Speech

What I taught teachers applies just as powerfully in life: Every environment has a **genetic code**—and words are the base pairs. Just like DNA strands form the code for life, your words and beliefs are forming the blueprint for your life.

In your home, your workplace, your mind—what you speak becomes the script. And once it's spoken, it begins coding your next behavior, your next emotion, your next outcome.

Your life isn't random. It's voice-activated.

From Reaction to Creation

Most people live in "reaction mode"—responding to stress, echoing complaints, repeating patterns inherited from childhood or past pain. But when you understand the power of your words, you shift into creation mode.

Creation mode says:

▶ "I may be surrounded by chaos, but I speak peace."
▶ "I see lack, but I declare abundance."
▶ "I feel fear, but I call courage forward."

This isn't wishful thinking. It's **neuroplasticity** in action. The more you speak intentional, life-producing words, the more your brain rewires itself to match that reality. New neural pathways are formed. Old cycles are disrupted. Your life begins to mirror the messages you consistently voice.

You stop reliving your history. And you start creating your future.

The Voice Audit

Pause. What have you been saying lately?

Make no mistake—your words are steering your life, whether you're paying attention or not. So before we go further, here's your first assignment:

Audit Your Voice.

Write down five phrases you've said consistently this week.

Then ask: Are these building the life I want—or the life I'm trying to escape?

Voice-Activated Living Starts Now

This is not about toxic positivity. It's about *conscious creation*. It's about reclaiming your voice from autopilot and using it as the instrument it was designed to be—a force for healing, alignment, peace, joy, faith, direction, and destiny.

You've spent years letting life speak to you. Now it's time for you to speak to life.

In the chapters that follow, we'll explore how your words shape your identity, influence your relationships, impact your physical and emotional health, and even create ripple effects for generations. But it starts here, in this moment, with this truth:

Your voice holds the code.

And the life you want is waiting to be activated.

Welcome to The Voice-Activated Life. Let's begin speaking the life you were meant to live.

NOTES

Bandura, A. (1997). *Self-Efficacy: The Exercise of Control*. W.H. Freeman.

Baumeister, R. F., Campbell, J. D., Krueger, J. I., & Vohs, K. D. (2003). Does high self-esteem cause better performance, interpersonal success, happiness, or healthier lifestyles? *Psychological Science in the Public Interest*, 4(1), 1–44.

Boaler, J. (2016). *Mathematical Mindsets: Unleashing Students' Potential through Creative Math, Inspiring Messages and Innovative Teaching*. Jossey-Bass.

Bower, S. A. (2004). *The Power of Positive Words: Transform Your Language, Transform Your Life*. New York: Wiley.

Brown, B. (2010). *The Gifts of Imperfection: Let Go of Who You Think You're Supposed to Be and Embrace Who You Are*. Hazelden Publishing.

Clear, J. (2018). *Atomic habits: An Easy & Proven Way To Build Good Habits & Break Bad Ones*. Avery.

Csikszentmihalyi, M. (1990). *Flow: The Psychology of Optimal Experience*. Harper & Row.

Davidson, R. J., & Begley, S. (2012). *The Emotional Life Of Your Brain: How Its Unique Patterns Affect The Way You Think, Feel, And Live—And How You Can Change Them*. Hudson Street Press.

Durlak, J. A., Weissberg, R. P., Dymnicki, A. B., Taylor, R. D., & Schellinger, K. B. (2011). *The impact of enhancing students' social and emotional learning: A meta-analysis of school-based universal interventions. Child Development*, 82(1), 405–432.

Dweck, C. S. (2006). *Mindset: The New Psychology of Success*. Random House.

Emoto, Masaru. *The True Power of Water: Healing and Discovering the Hidden Secrets of Water*. Hado Publishing, 2013.

Fullan, M. (2014). *The Principal: Three Keys to Maximizing Impact*. Jossey-Bass.

Fredrickson, B. L. (2001). The role of positive emotions in positive psychology: The broaden-and-build theory of positive emotions. *American Psychologist*, 56(3), 218–226.

Gay, G. (2010). *Culturally Responsive Teaching: Theory, Research, and Practice.* Teachers College Press.

Hart, B., & Risley, T. R. (1995). *Meaningful differences in the everyday experience of young American children.* Baltimore, MD: Paul H. Brookes Publishing Co.

Harter, S. (2012). *The Construction of the Self: Developmental and Sociocultural Foundations.* Guilford Press.

Hattie, J. (2009). *Visible Learning: A Synthesis of Over 800 Meta-Analyses Relating to Achievement.* Routledge.

Hattie, J., & Timperley, H. (2007). The power of feedback. *Review of Educational Research*, 77(1), 81–112.

Howard-Jones, P. (2007). *Neuroscience and Education: A Review.* York: Research Evidence in Education Library.

Immordino-Yang, M. H., & Damasio, A. (2007). *We Feel, Therefore We Learn: The Relevance of Affective and Social Neuroscience to Education.* Mind, Brain, and Education, 1(1), 3–10. https://doi.org/10.1111/j.1751-228X.2007.00004.x

Jensen, E. (2009). *Teaching with Poverty in Mind: What Being Poor Does to Kids' Brains and What Schools Can Do About It.* ASCD.

Jones, S. M., & Kahn, J. (2017). *The evidence base for how we learn: Supporting students' social, emotional, and academic development.* National Commission on Social, Emotional, and Academic Development.

Ladson-Billings, G. (1995). Toward a theory of culturally relevant pedagogy. *American Educational Research Journal*, 32(3), 465–491.

Leithwood, K., Louis, K. S., Anderson, S., & Wahlstrom, K. (2004). *How leadership influences student learning.* The Wallace Foundation.

Marzano, R. J., Pickering, D. J., & Pollock, J. E. (2001). *Classroom Instruction That Works: Research-Based Strategies for Increasing Student Achievement.* ASCD.

Masten, A. S. (2014). *Ordinary Magic: Resilience in Development.* Guilford Press.

National Geographic Society. (2021). *The Water Cycle.* National Geographic, , www.nationalgeographic.org/encyclopedia/water-cycle/. Accessed 31 Aug. 2024.

Newberg, A., & Waldman, M. R. (2012). *Words Can Change Your Brain: 12 Conversation Strategies to Build Trust, Resolve Conflict, and Increase Intimacy.* New York: Hudson Street Press.

Rattan, A., Good, C., & Dweck, C. S. (2012). "It's ok — Not everyone can be good at math": Instructors with an entity theory comfort (and demotivate) students. *Journal of Experimental Social Psychology*, 48(3), 731–737.

Rosenthal, R., & Jacobson, L. (1968). Pygmalion in the classroom: Teacher expectation and pupils' intellectual development. *The Urban Review*, 3(1), 16–20.

Sadker, M., & Sadker, D. (1994). *Failing at Fairness: How America's Schools Cheat Girls.* Simon & Schuster.

Skinner, B. F. (1953). *Science and human behavior.* New York, NY: Macmillan.

Ungar, M. (2011). *The Social Ecology of Resilience: A Handbook of Theory and Practice.* Springer.

Walker, K. A., & Jiang, X. (2022). An examination of the moderating role of growth mindset in the relation between social stress and externalizing behaviors among adolescents. *Journal of Adolescence*, 94, 1–10. https://doi.org/10.1002/jad.12006

Winner, E. (1996). *Gifted Children: Myths and Realities.* Basic Books.

Wong, H. K., & Wong, R. T. (2009). *The First Days of School: How to Be an Effective Teacher.* Harry K. Wong Publications.

ABOUT THE AUTHOR

DR. LAKESA B. MITCHELL is a wife and mother who enjoys eating her mother's gumbo, vacationing around the world, and worshipping. In her spare time, she has become a TEDx speaker, author, and Educational Neural Architect—passionate about teaching people how to rewire the brain with life-producing phrases to unlock potential and transform lives.

With over 30 years of experience in education, leadership, and personal development, she has dedicated her career to helping individuals and organizations reshape their mindsets and rewire their neural pathways, and empowering individuals through the strength of thoughts, words, and perspectives.

With an extensive 17-year background as a school principal across elementary, middle, and high school settings in both parochial and public schools, Dr. Mitchell has firsthand experience transforming school cultures, developing leadership strategies, and empowering educators, students, and families. As a professional speaker and consultant, she shares cutting-edge insights relating to Voice-Activation, resilience, and leadership to inspire audiences in education, corporate sectors, and faith-based communities.

Her expertise extends beyond education into real estate, ministry, and corporate leadership, making her a versatile and impactful speaker.

Invite LaKesa to speak with your team, school, student body or parent group: www.lakesabradfordmitchell.com

www.ingramcontent.com/pod-product-compliance
Lightning Source LLC
Chambersburg PA
CBHW071737120626
46550CB00002B/559